TURTLE

Coloring Book

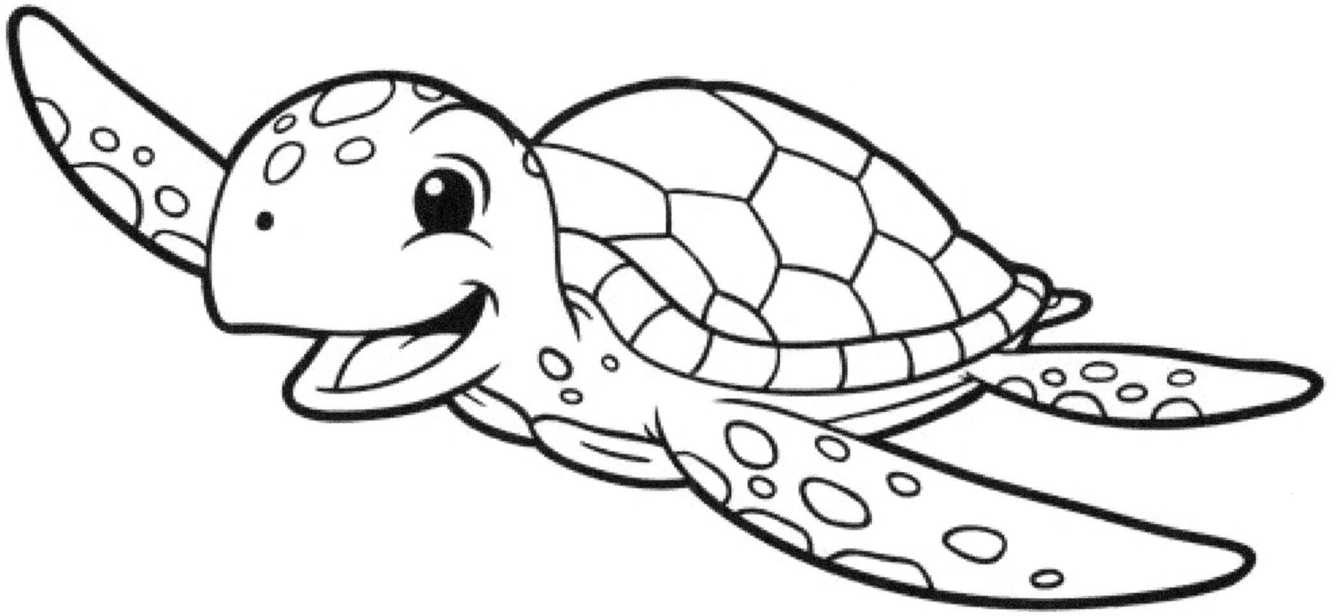

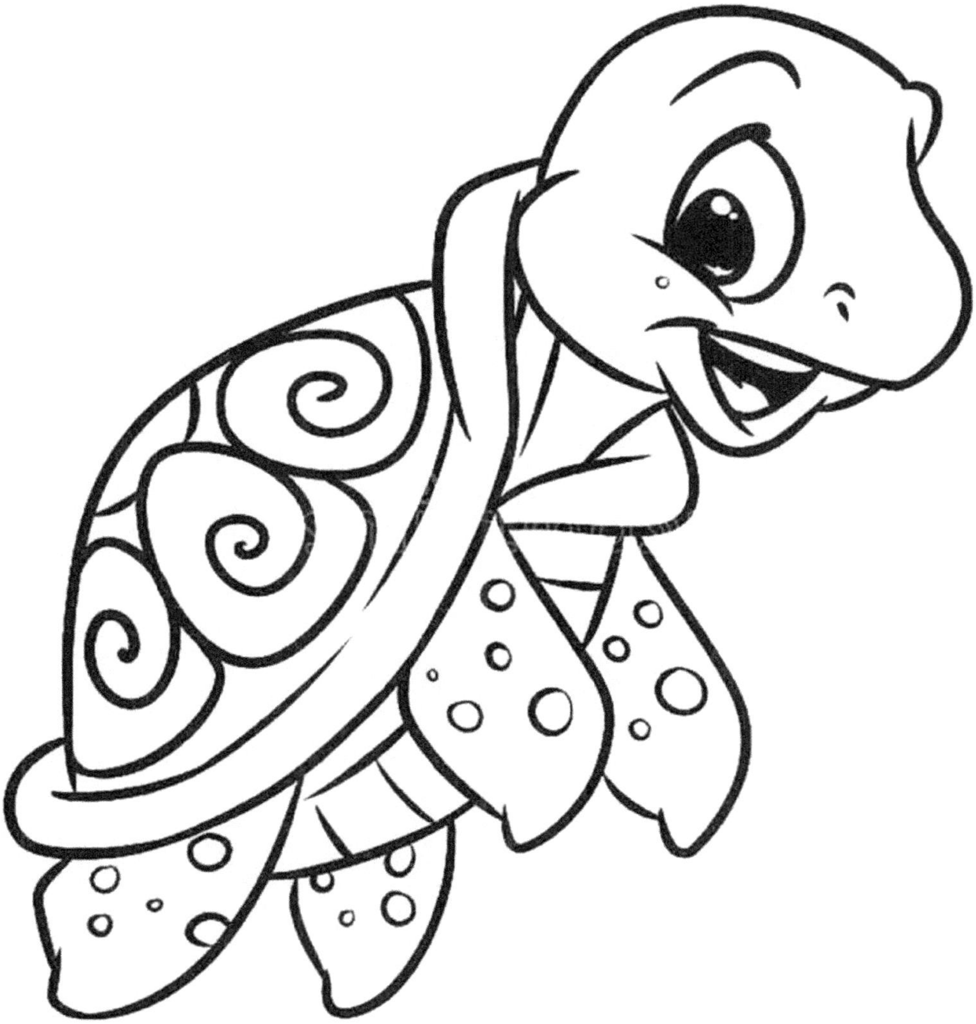

This book belongs to

____

____

TEST COLORING PAGE

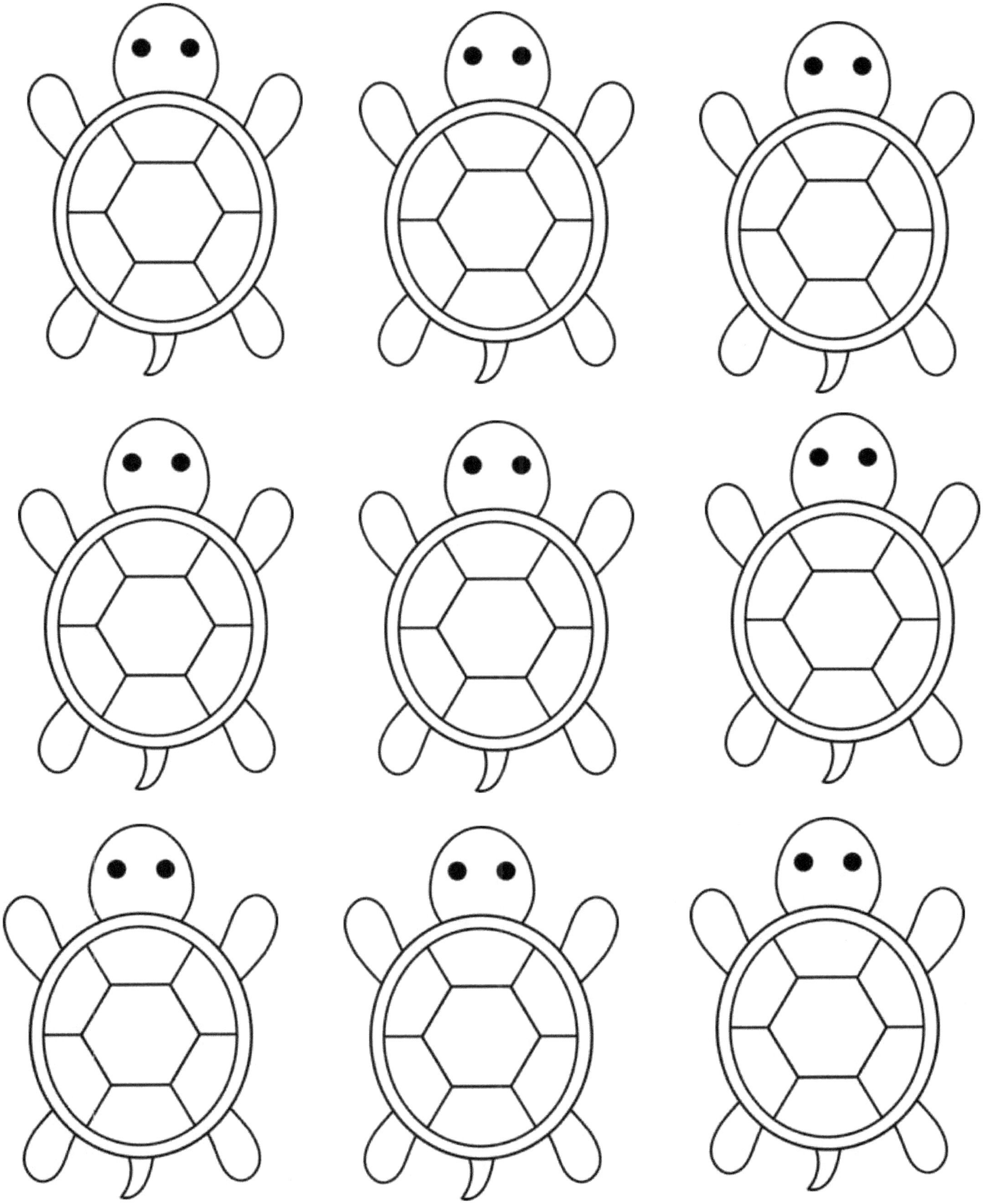

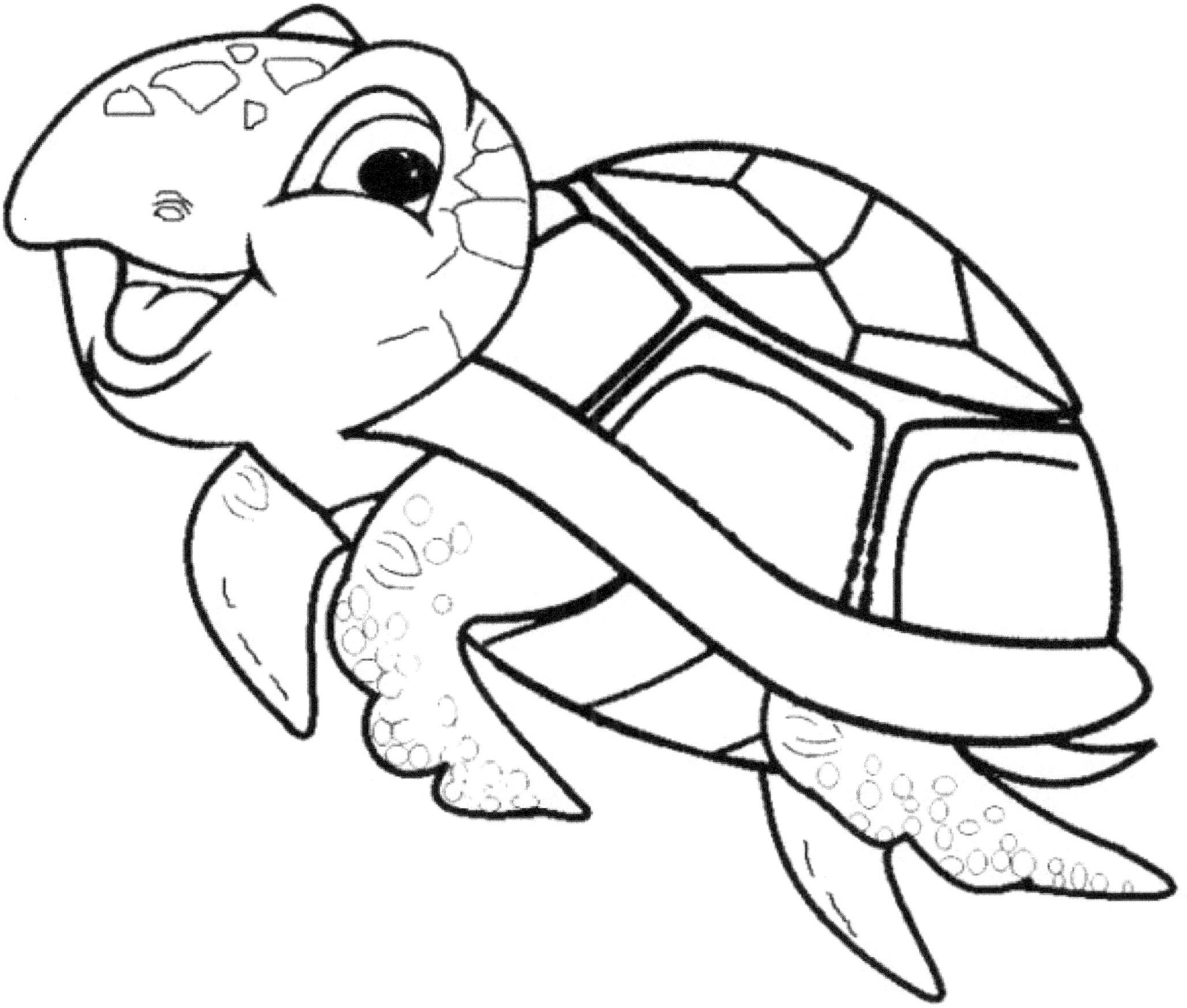

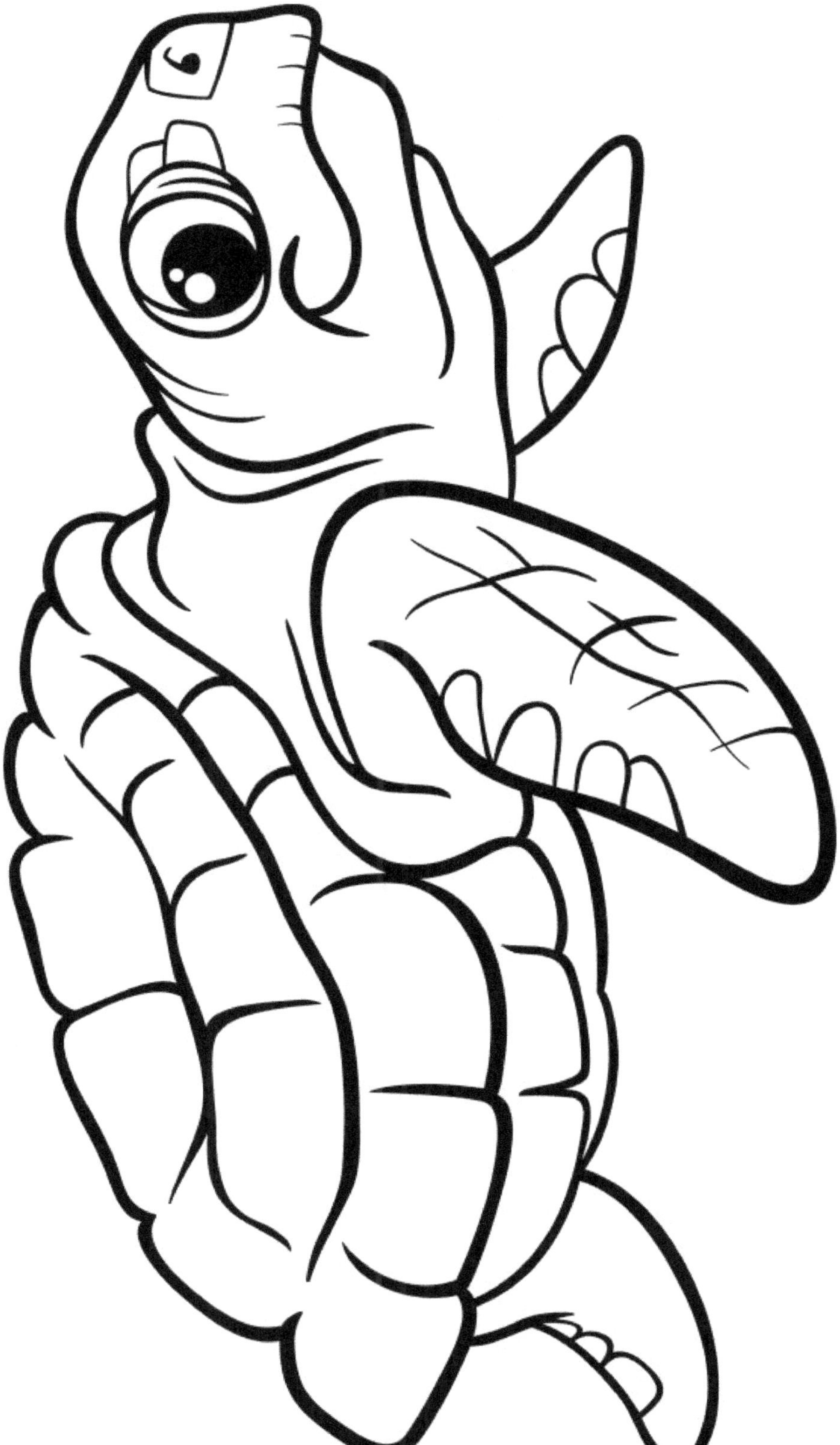

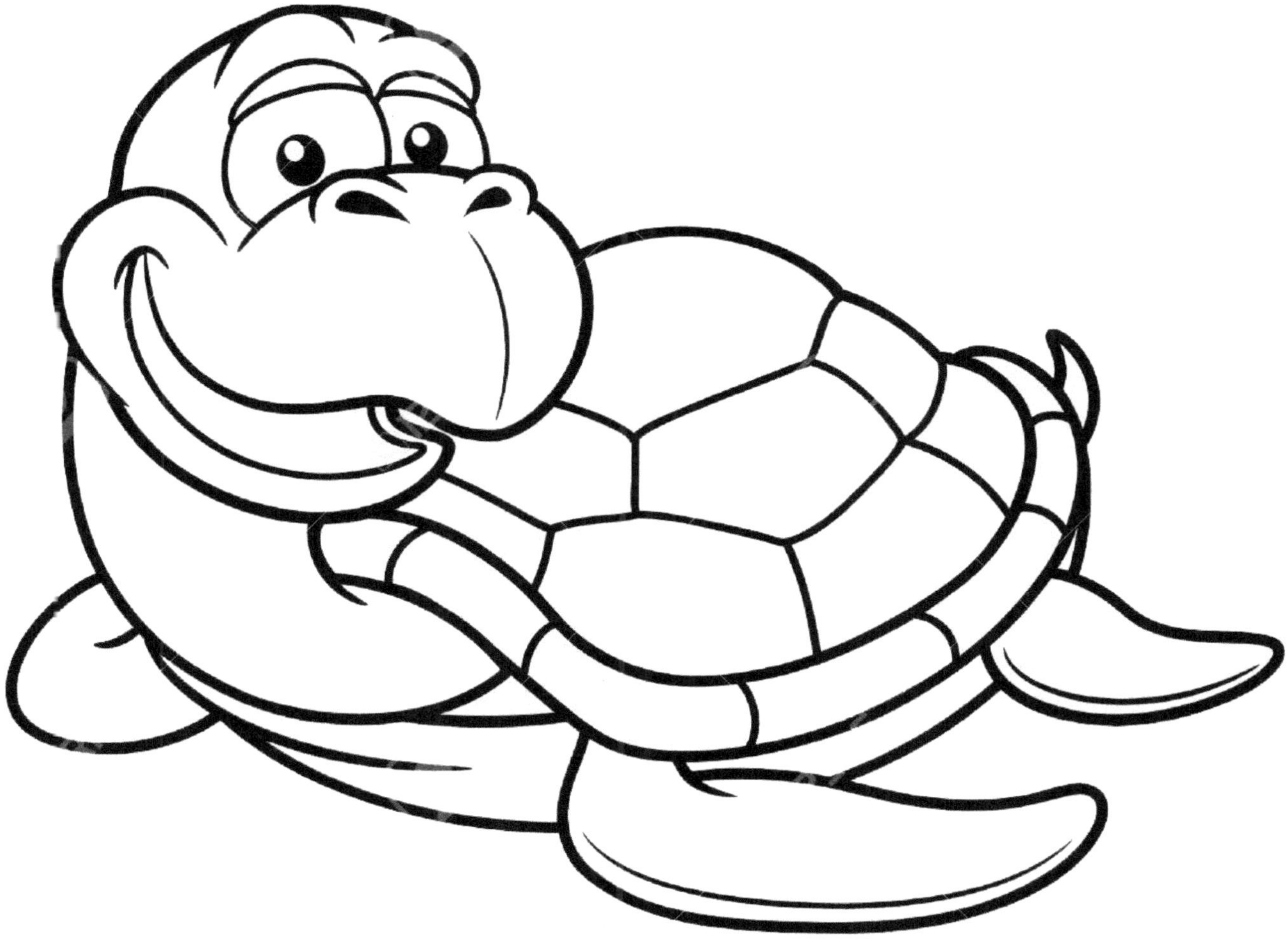

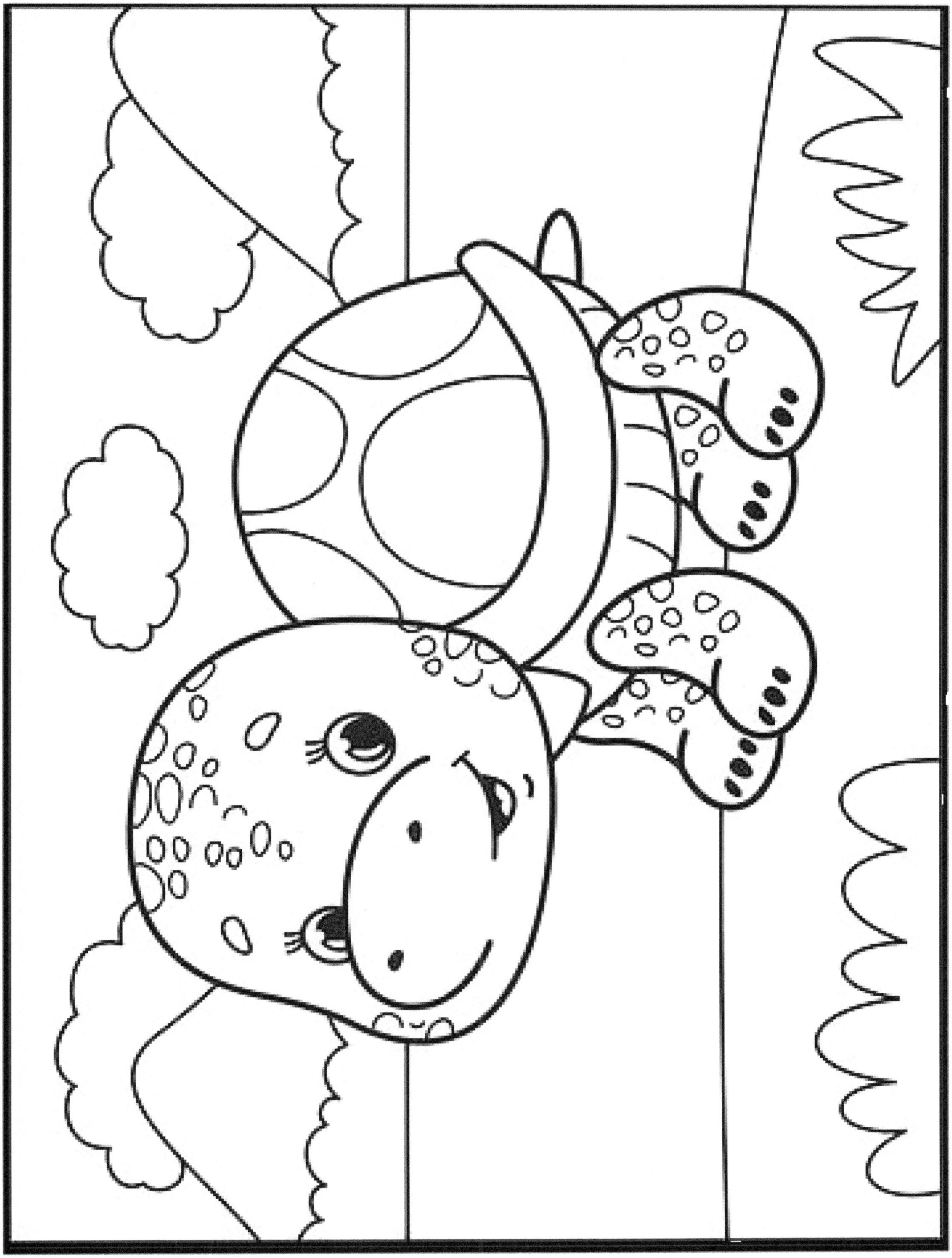

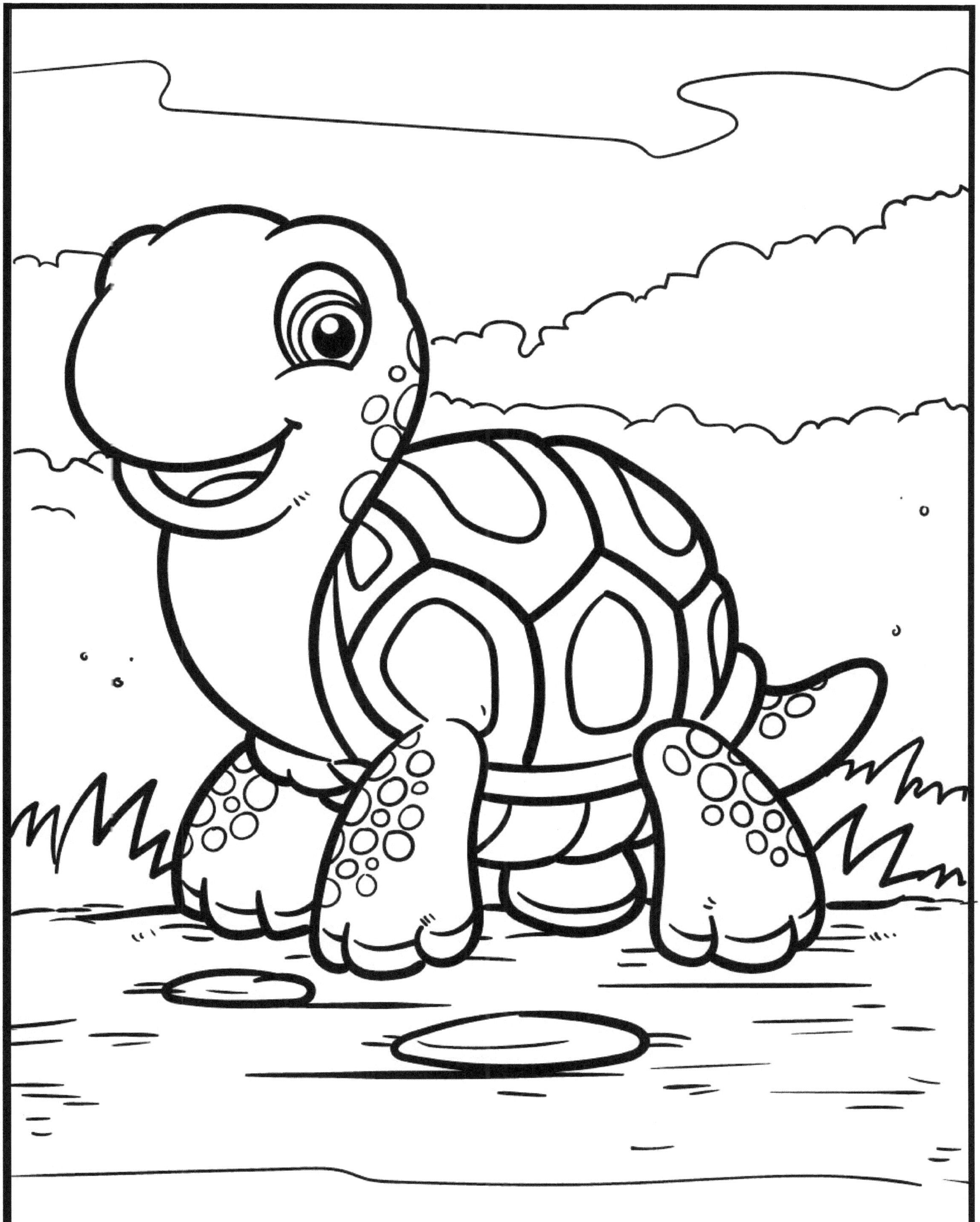

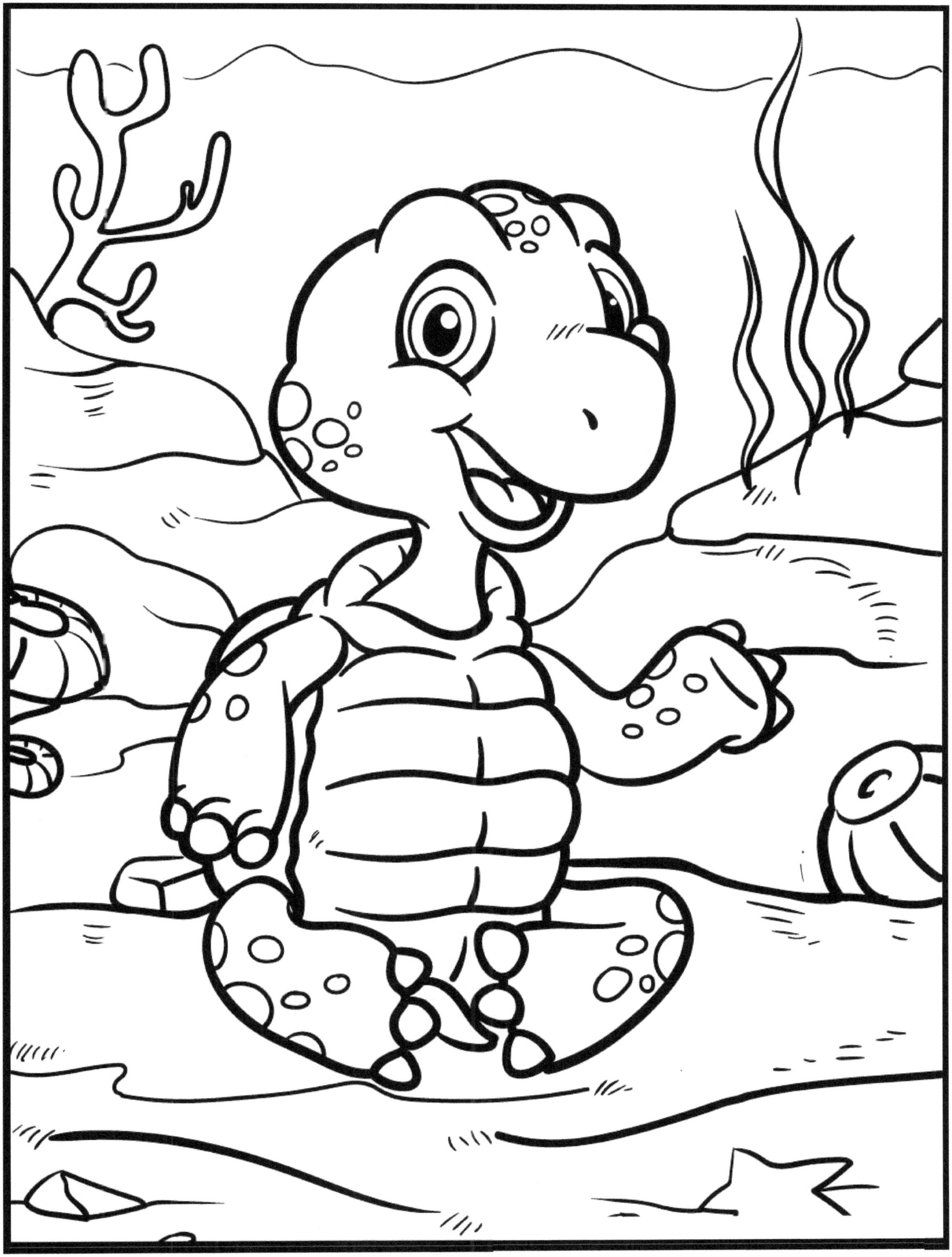

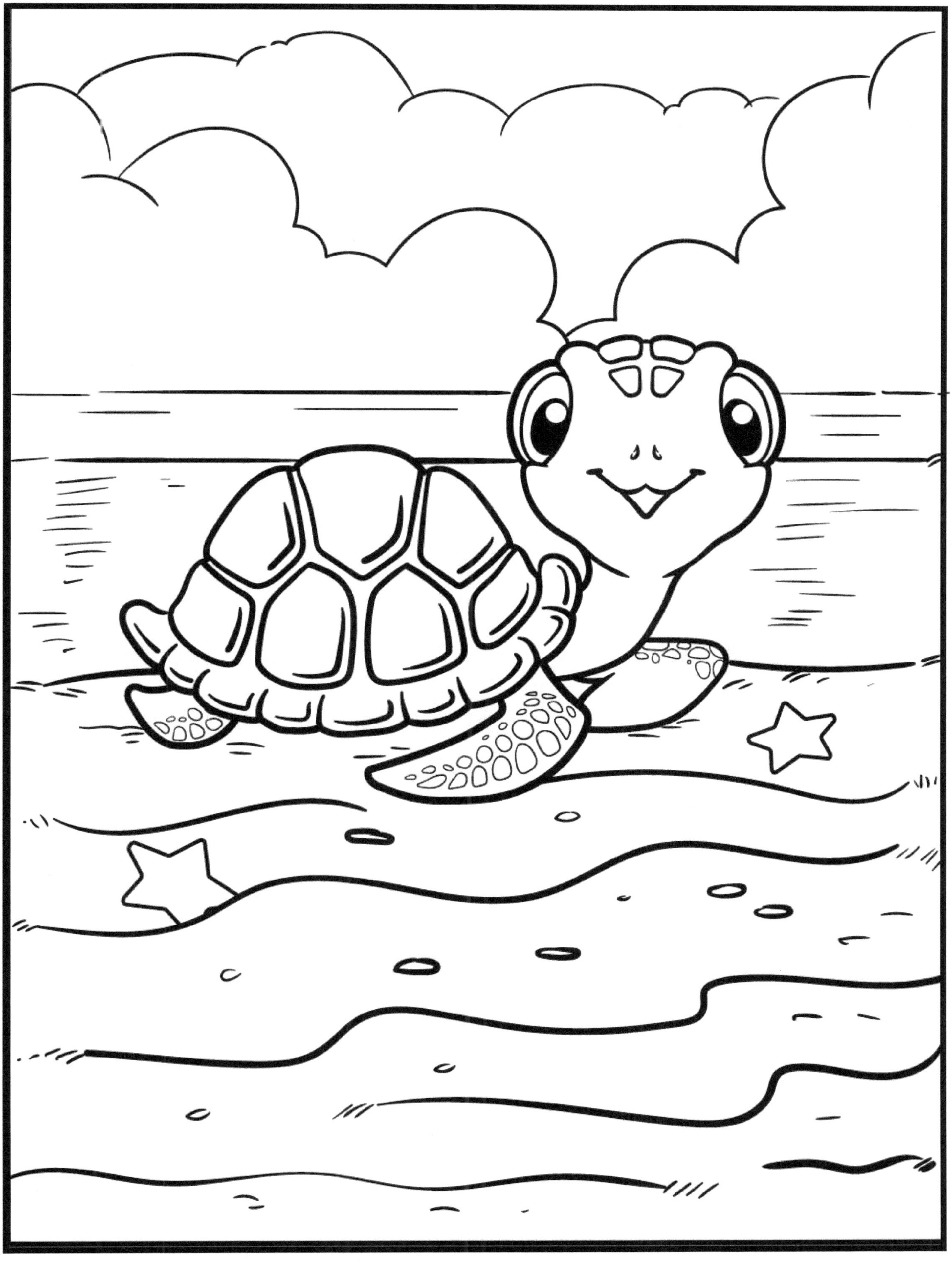

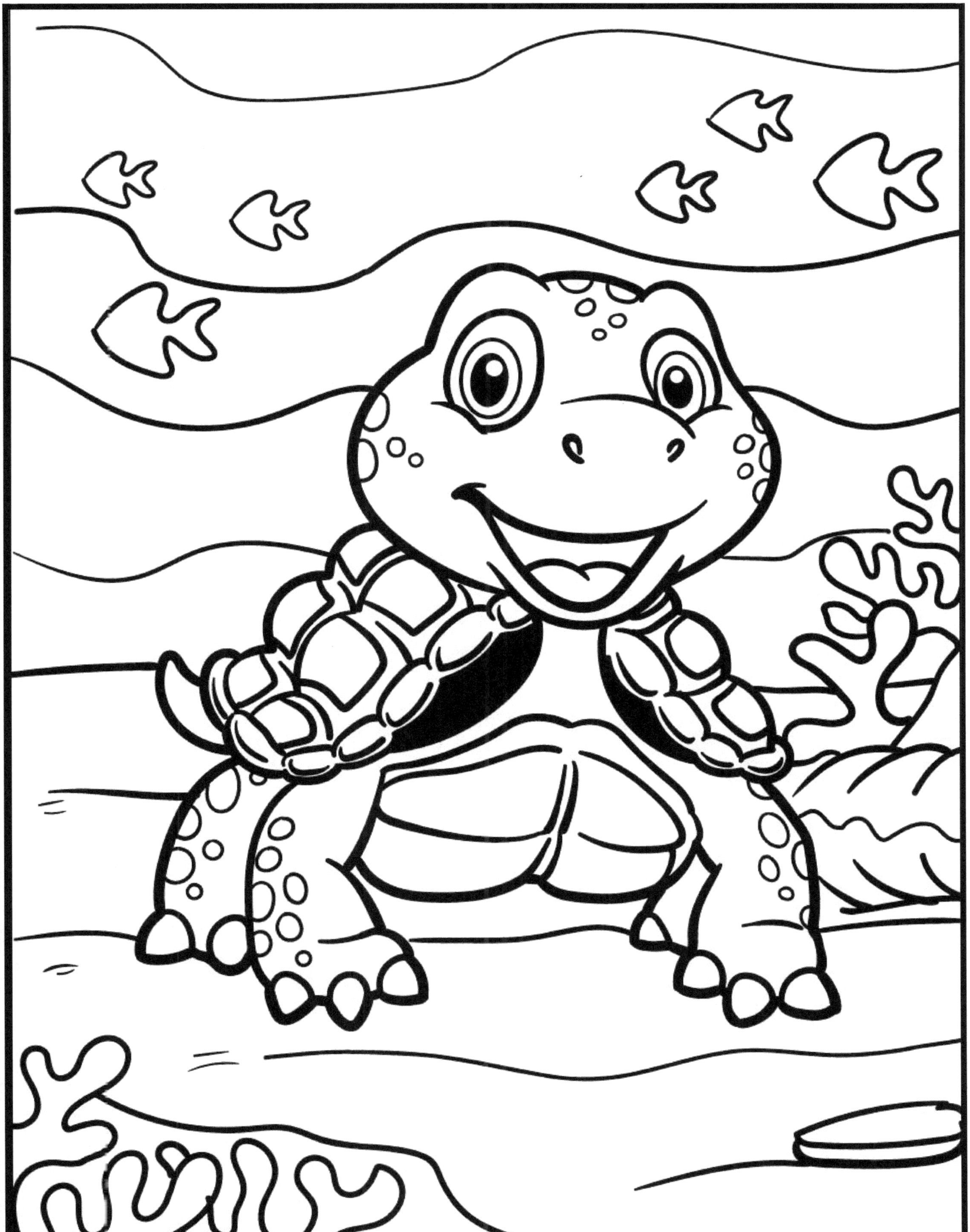

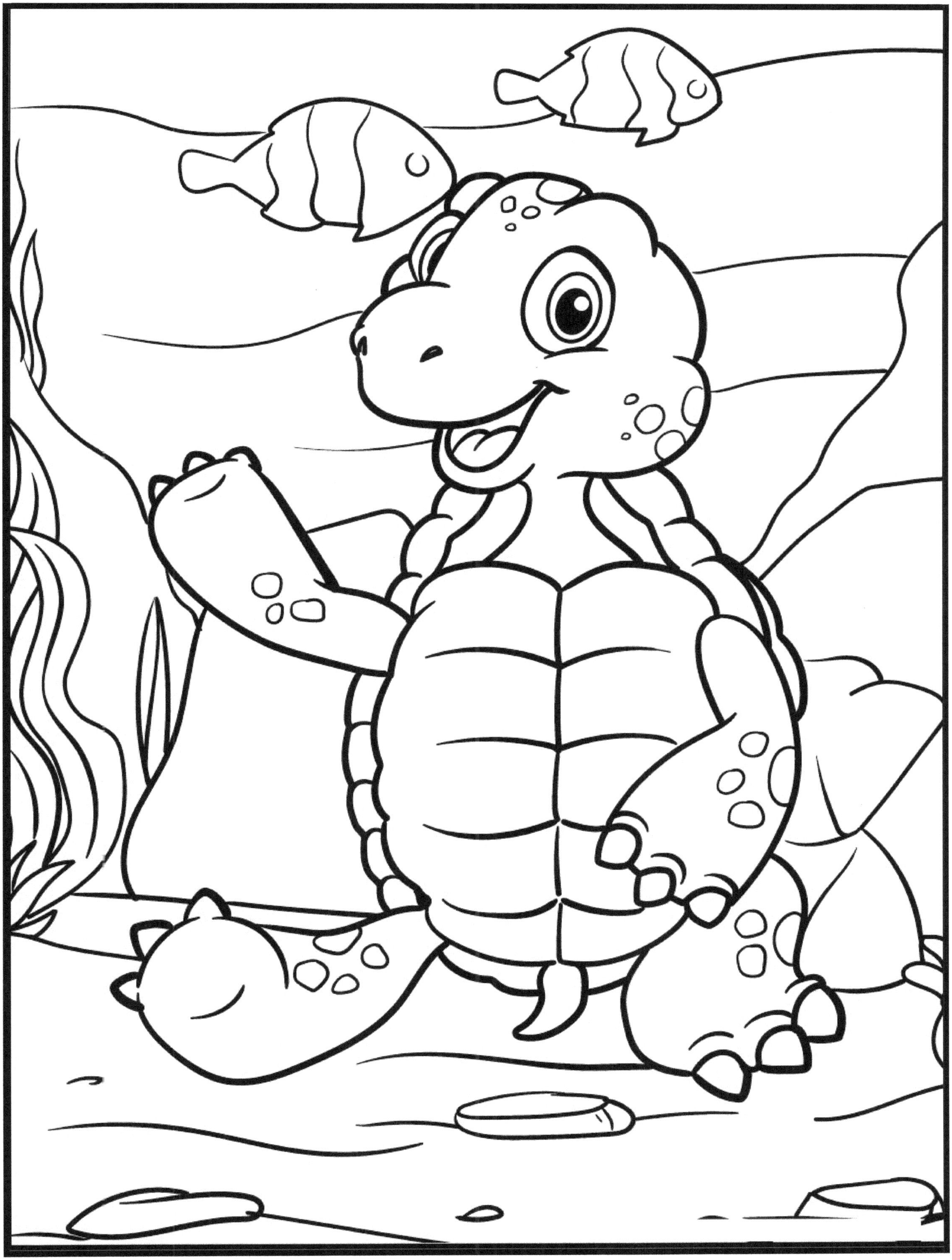

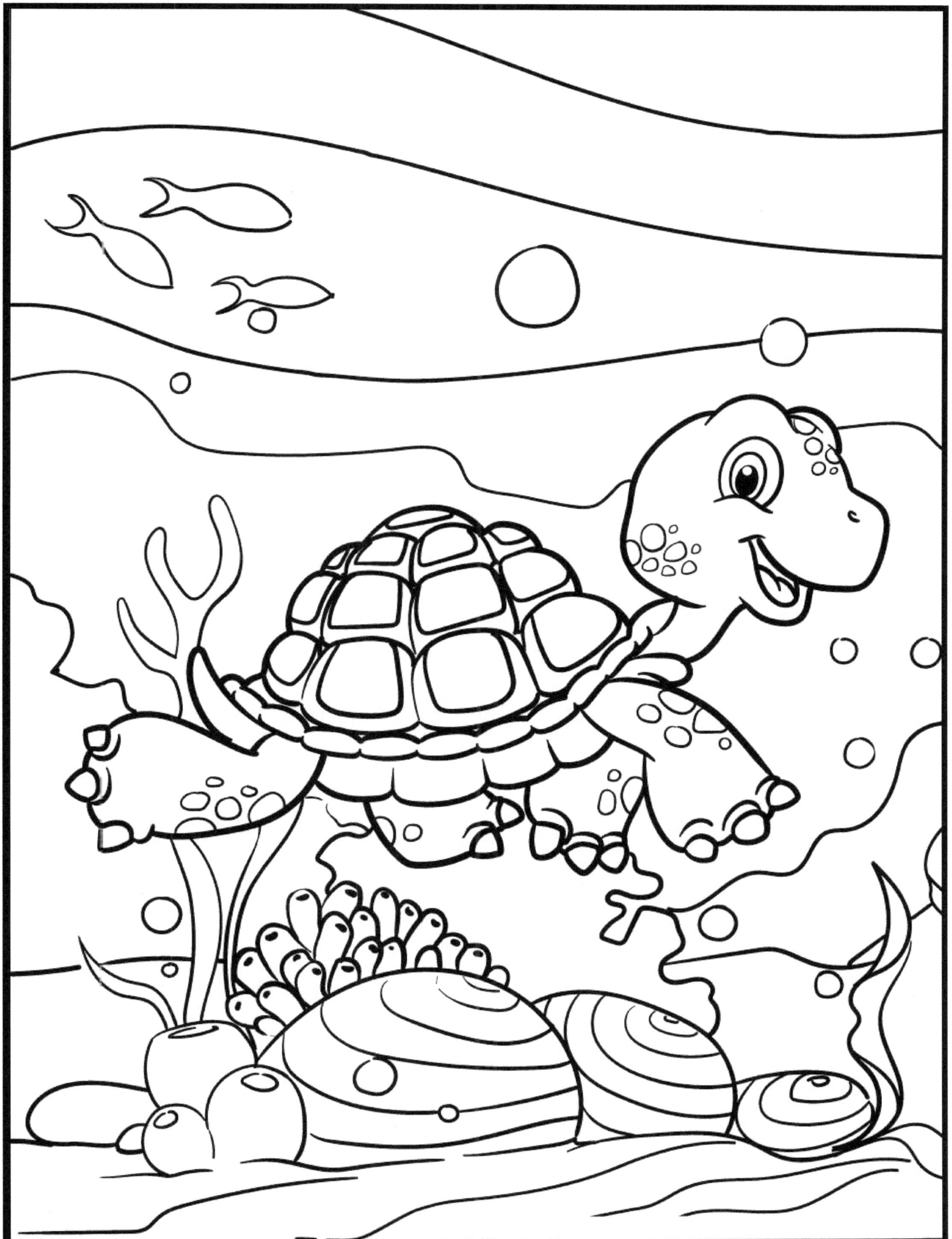

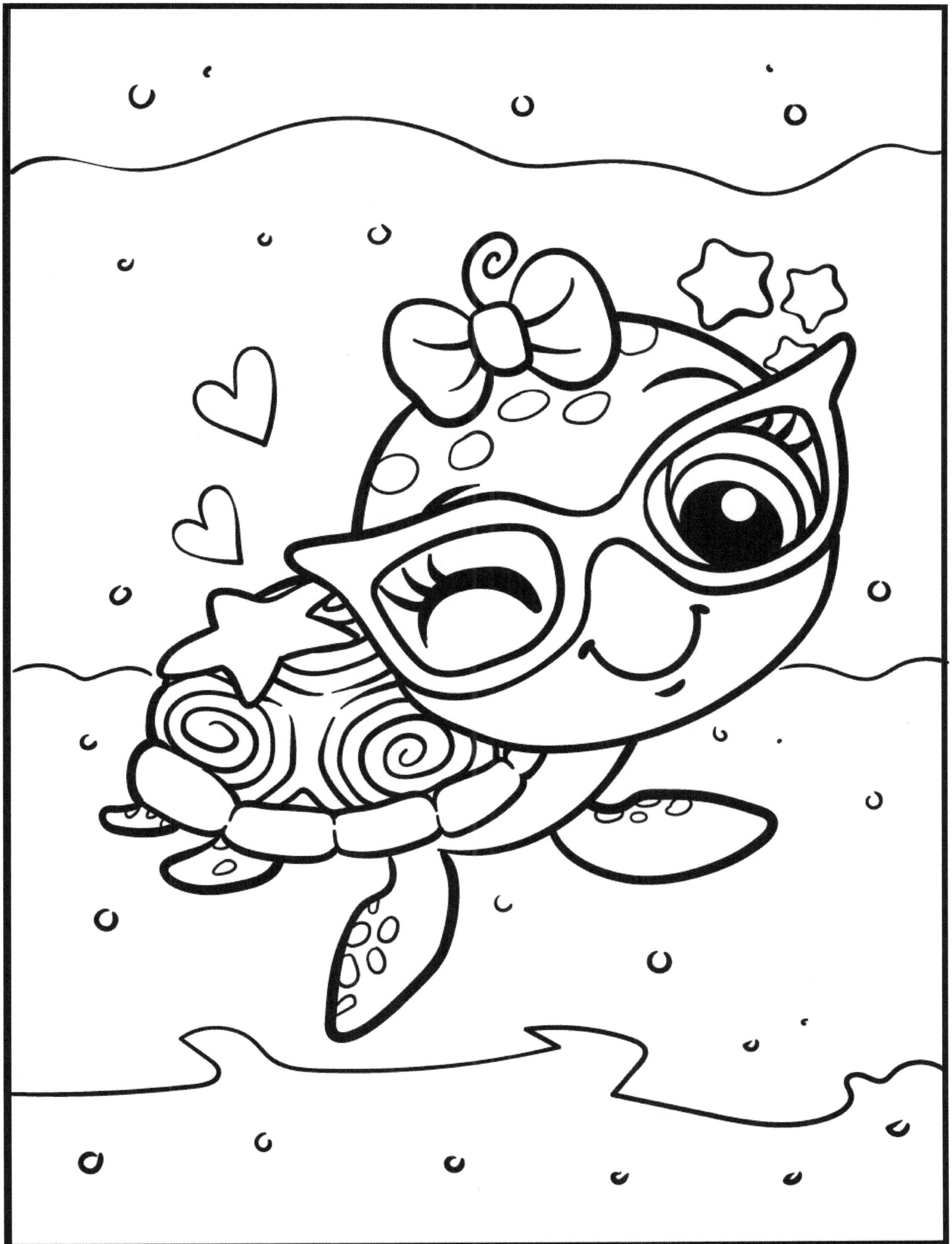

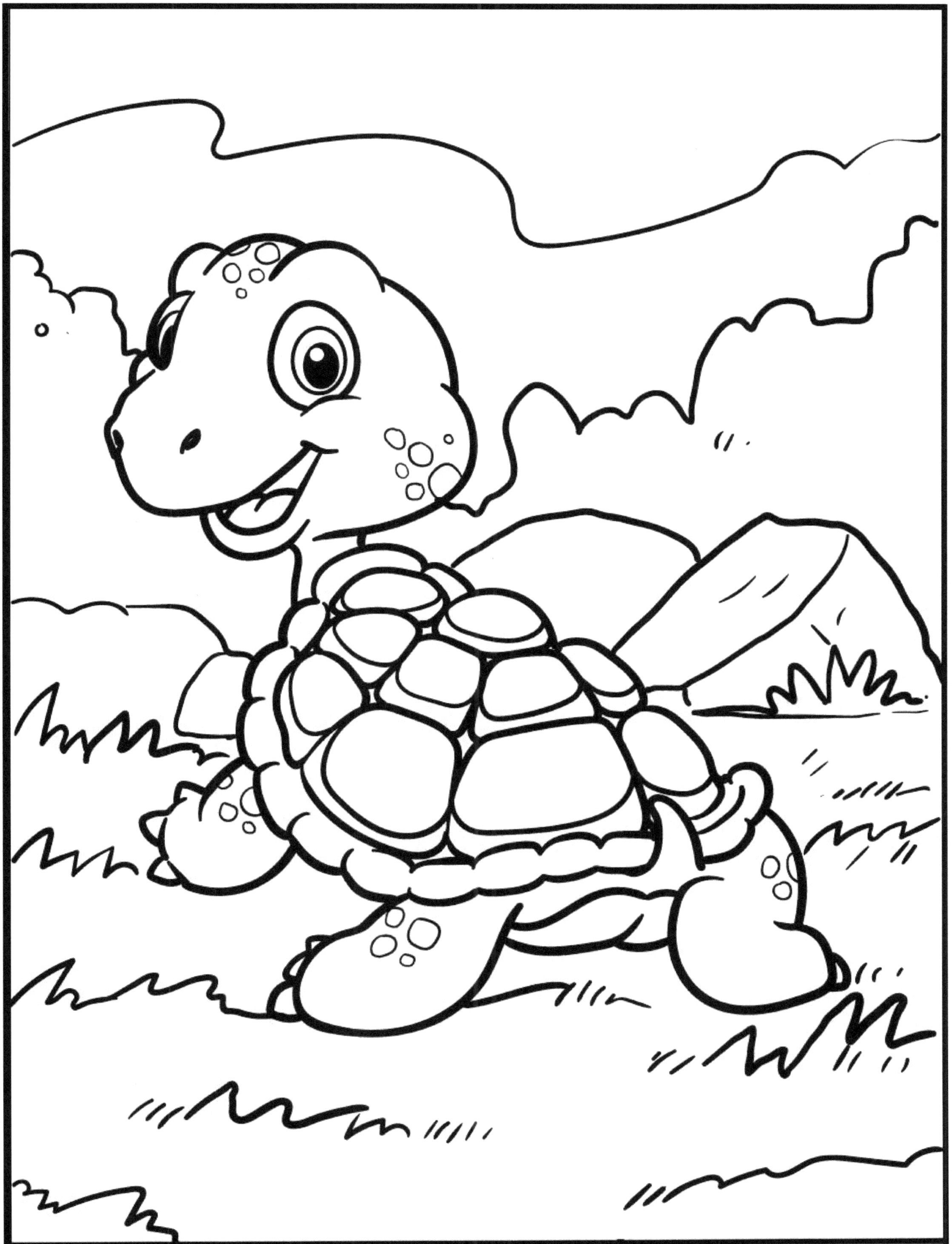

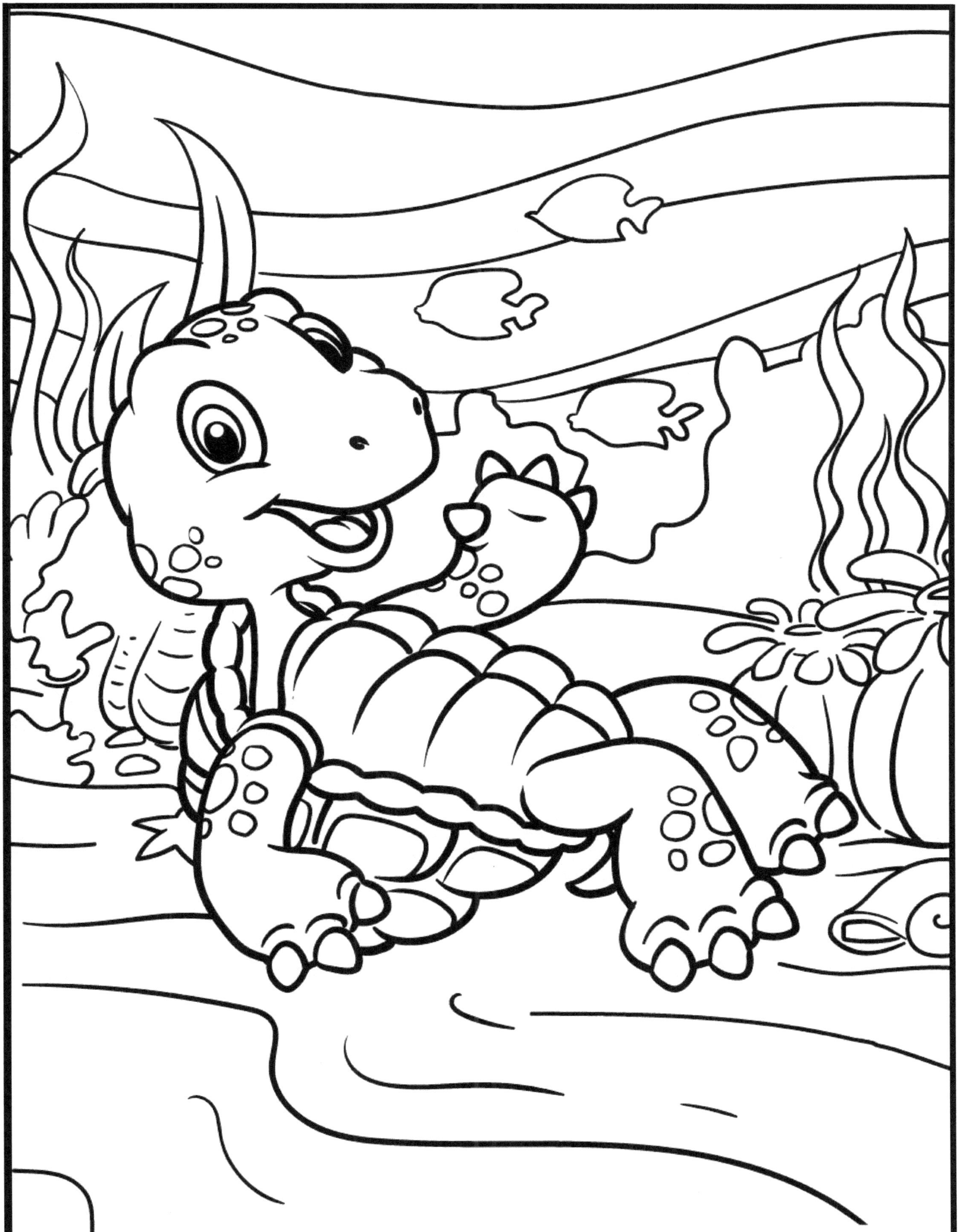

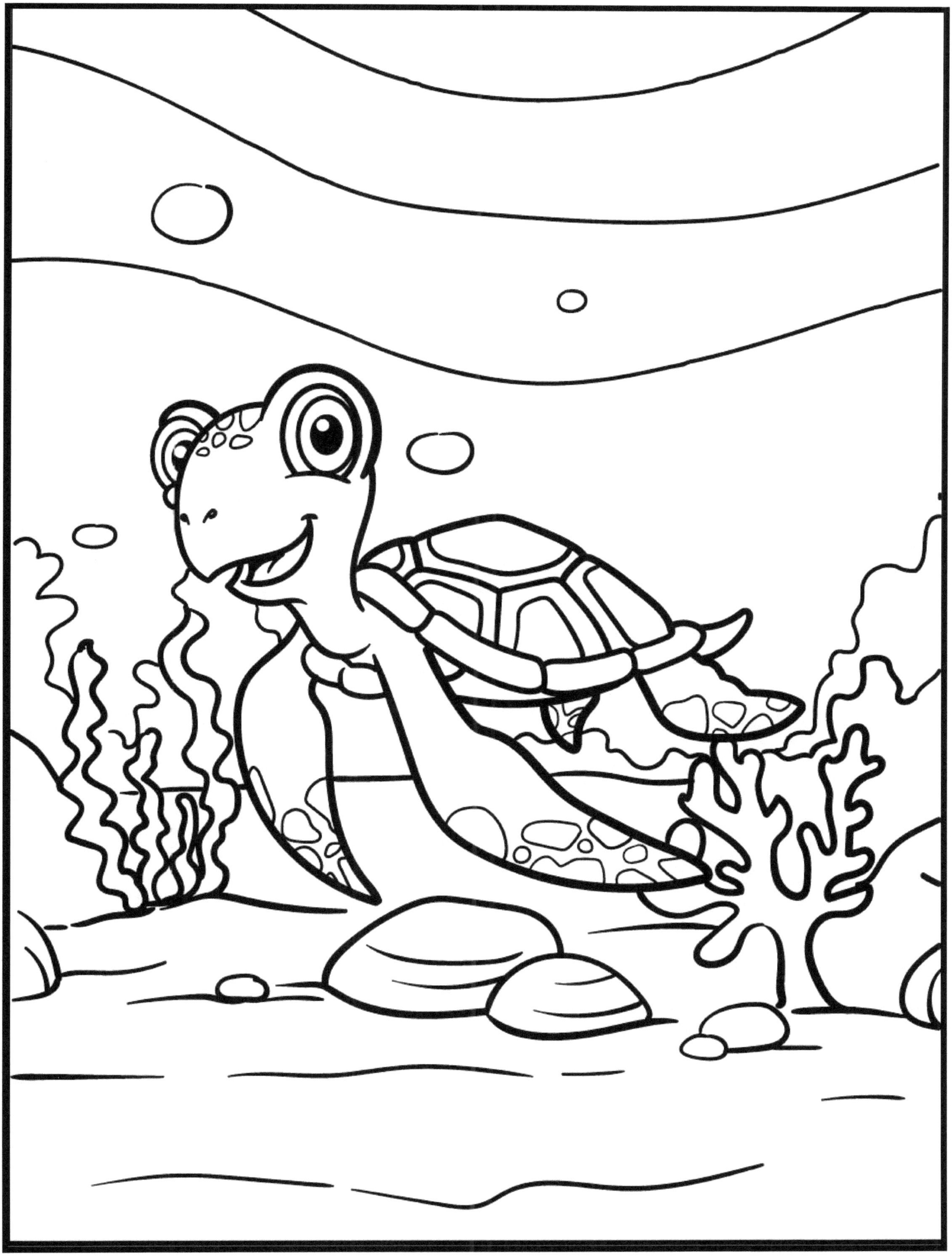

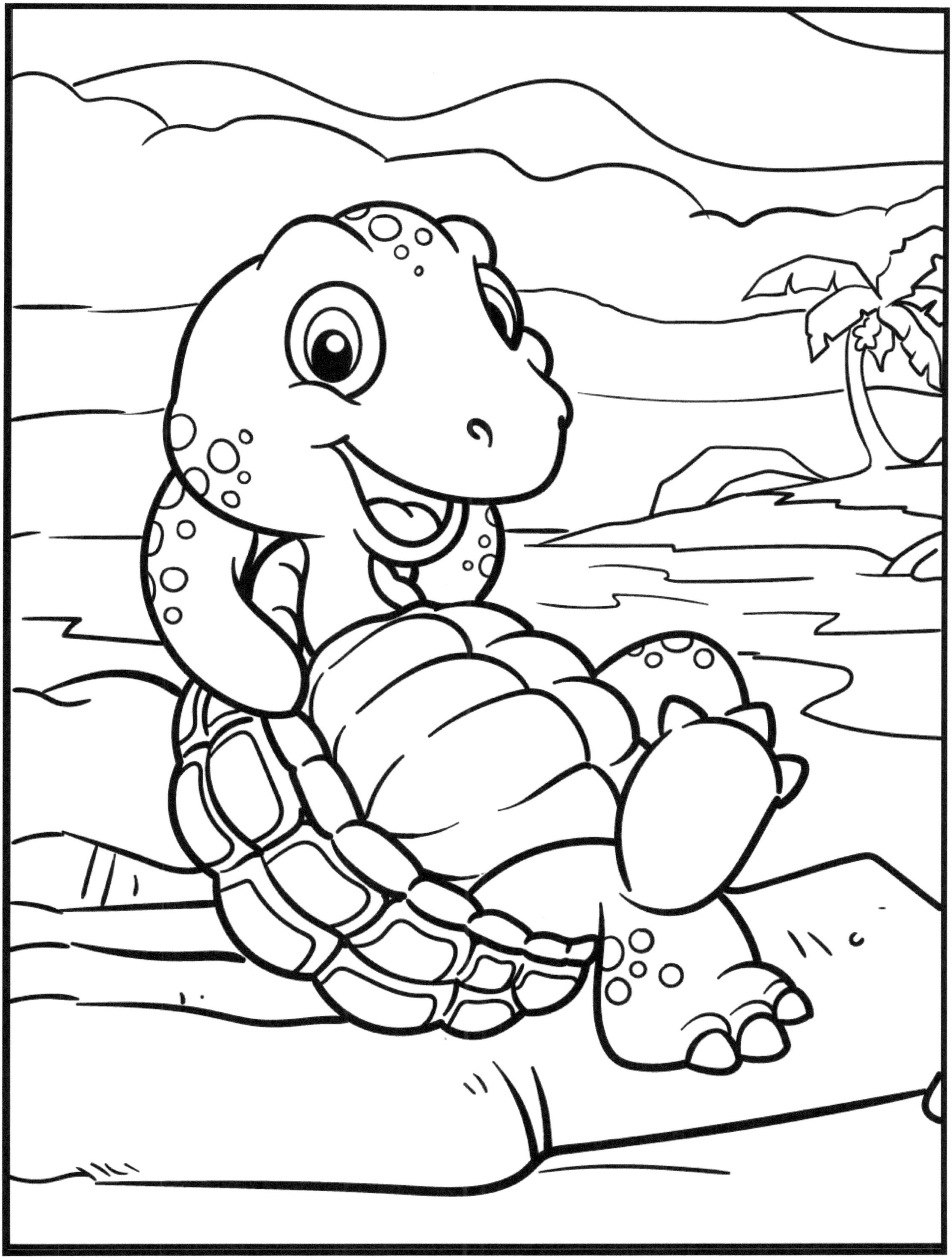

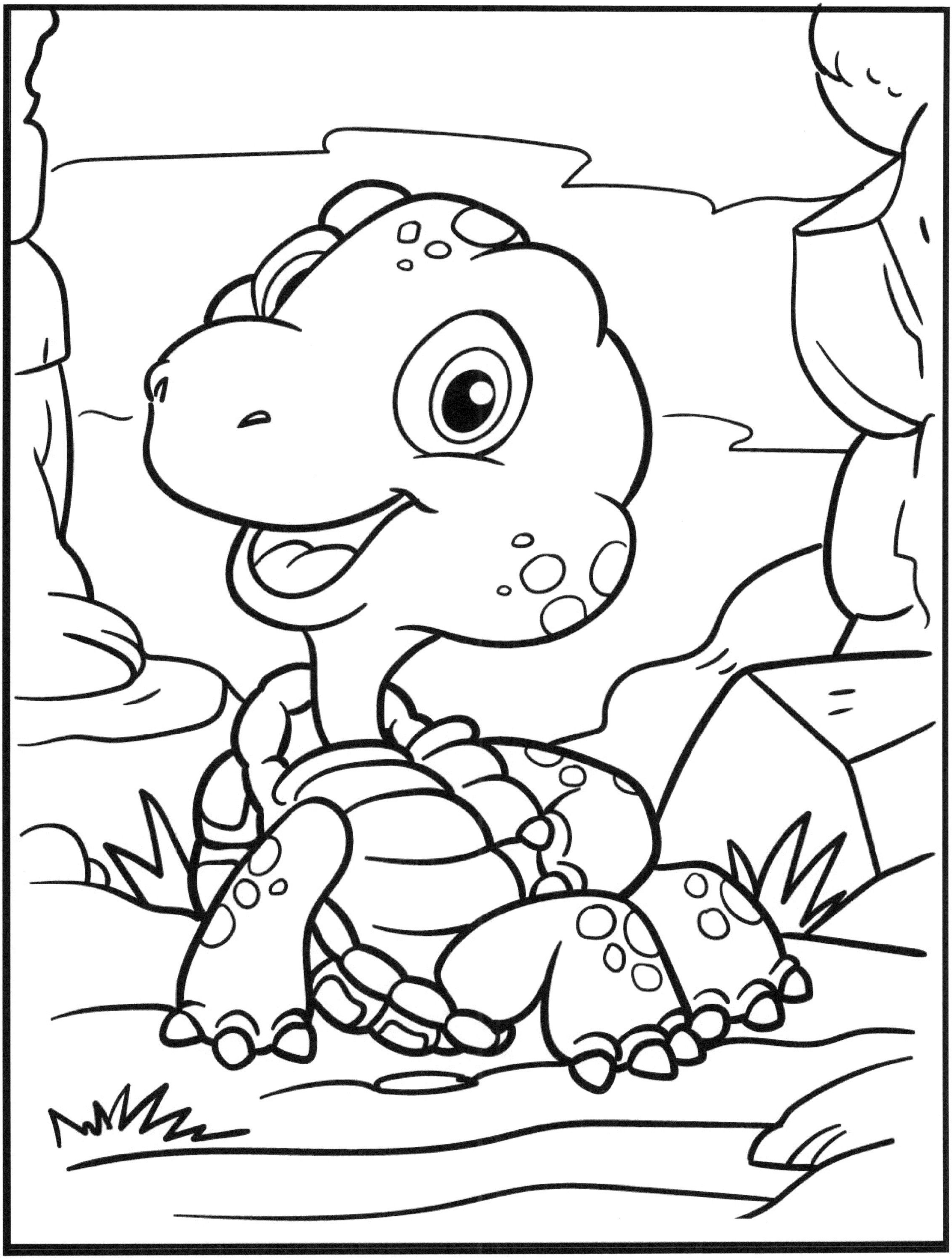

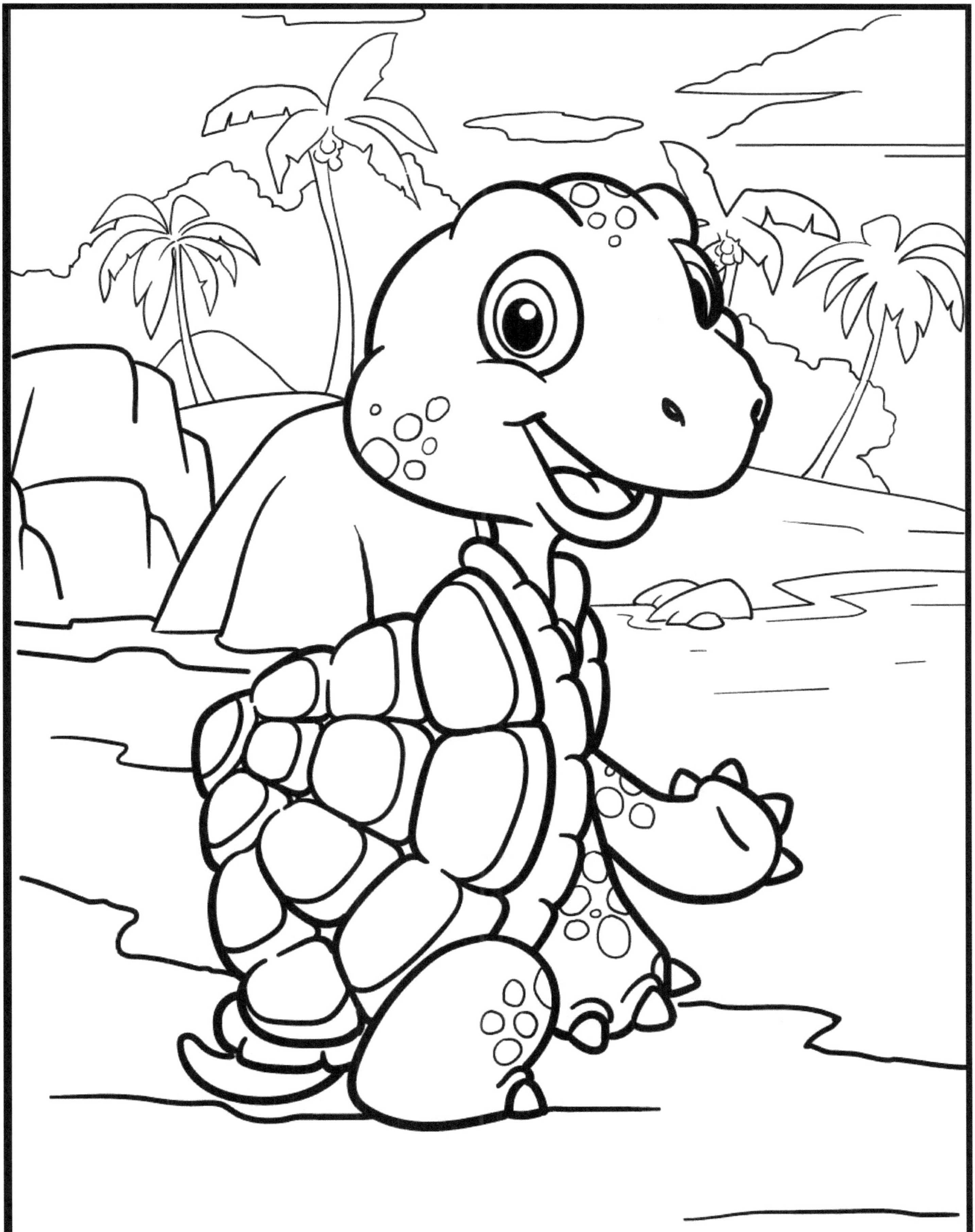

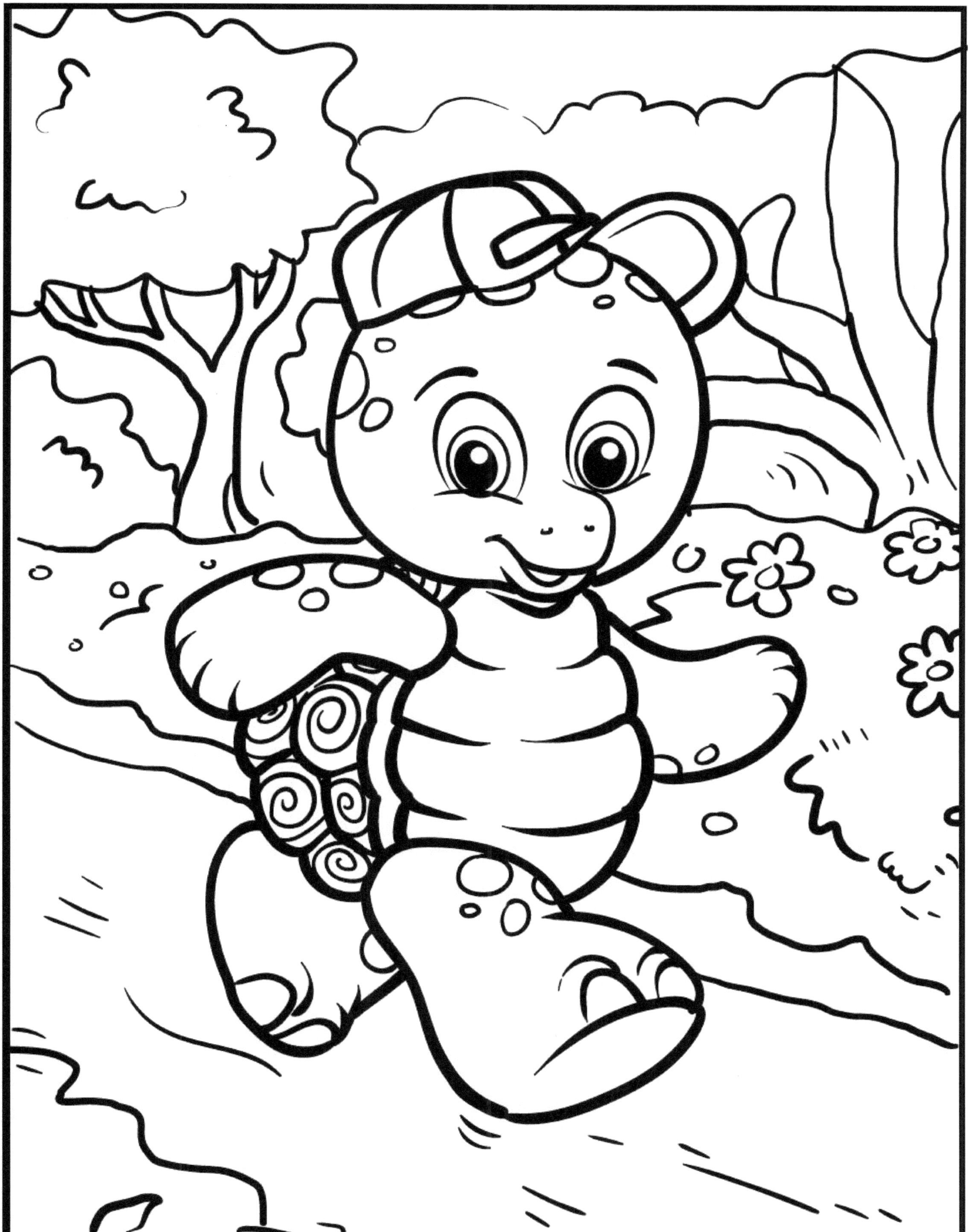

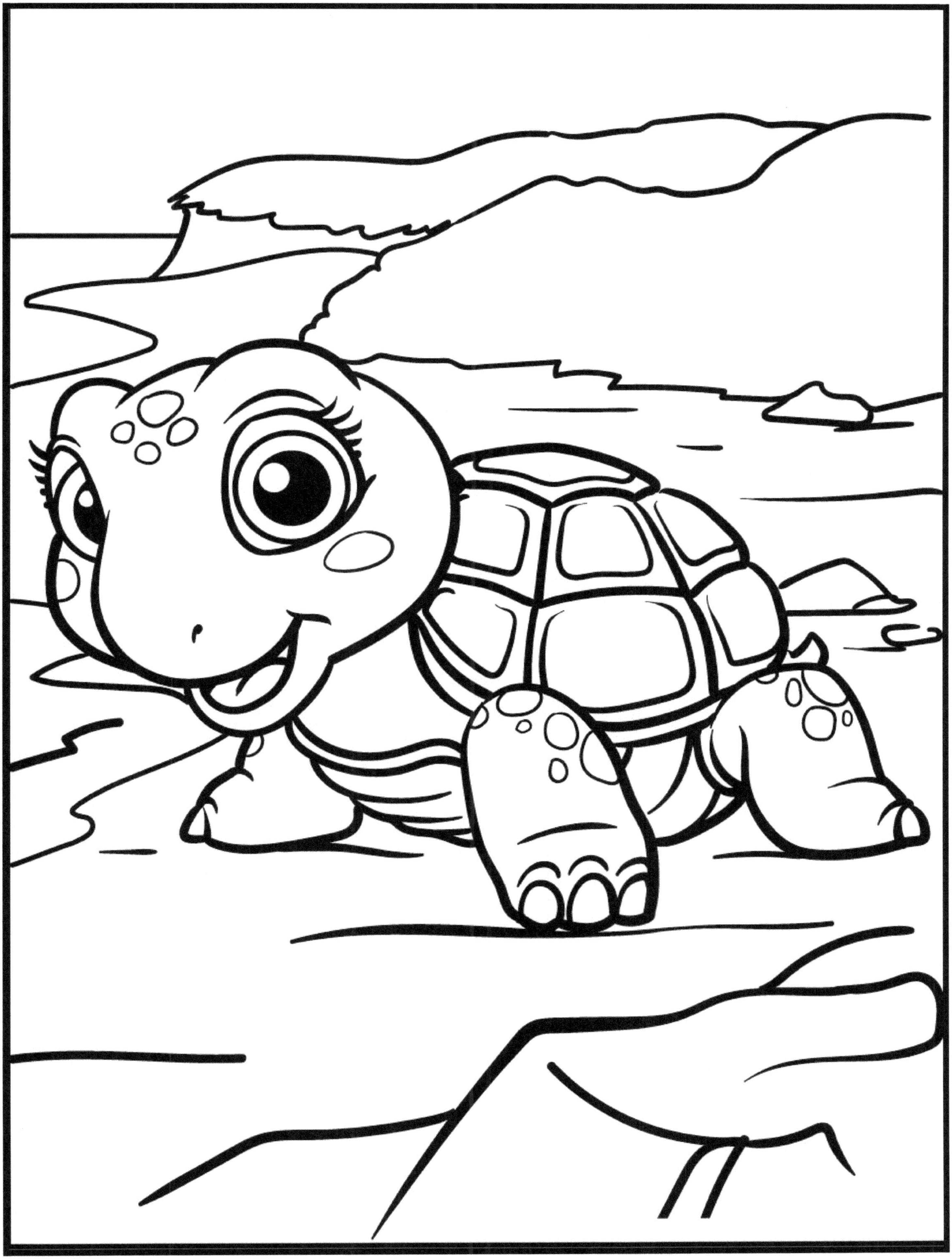

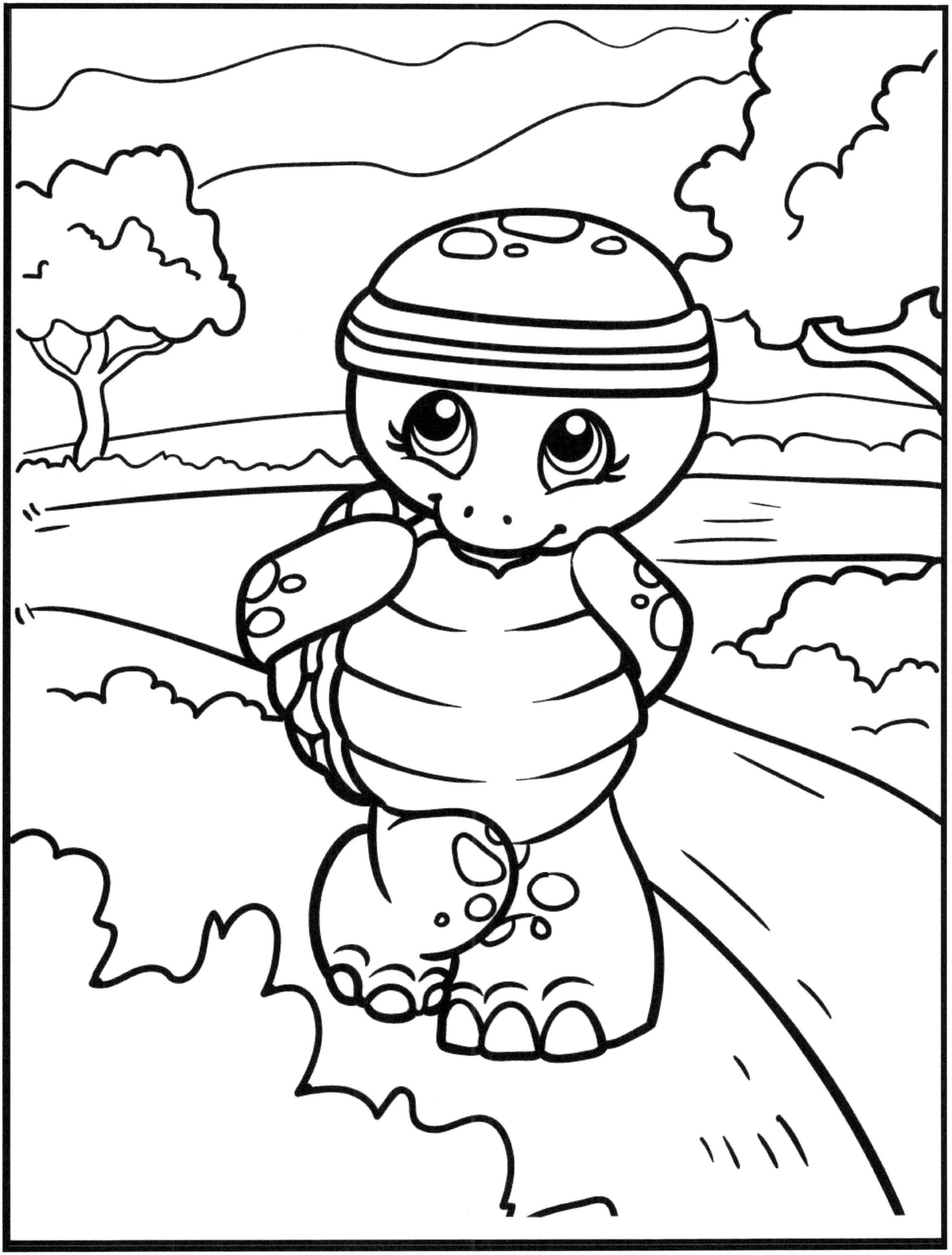

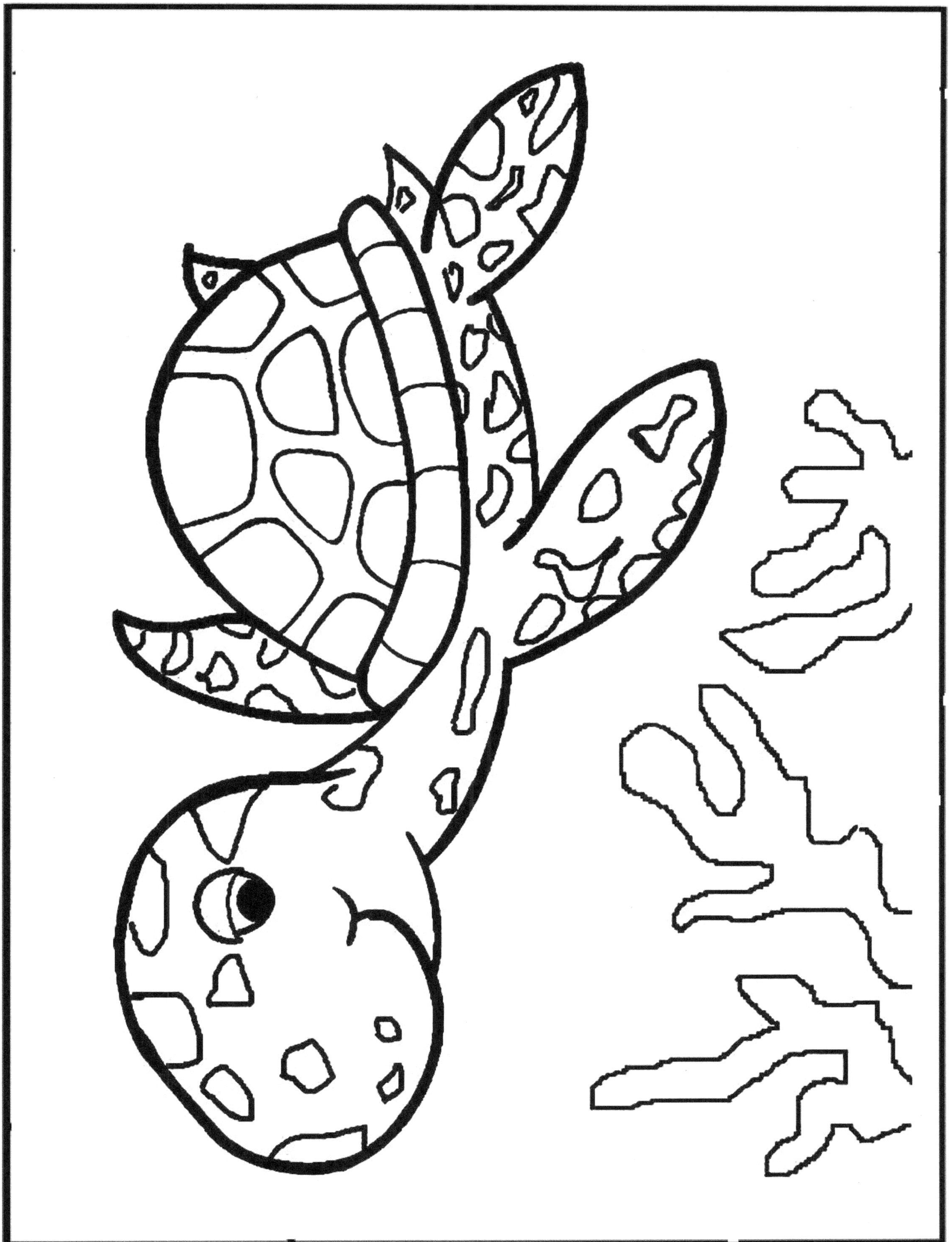

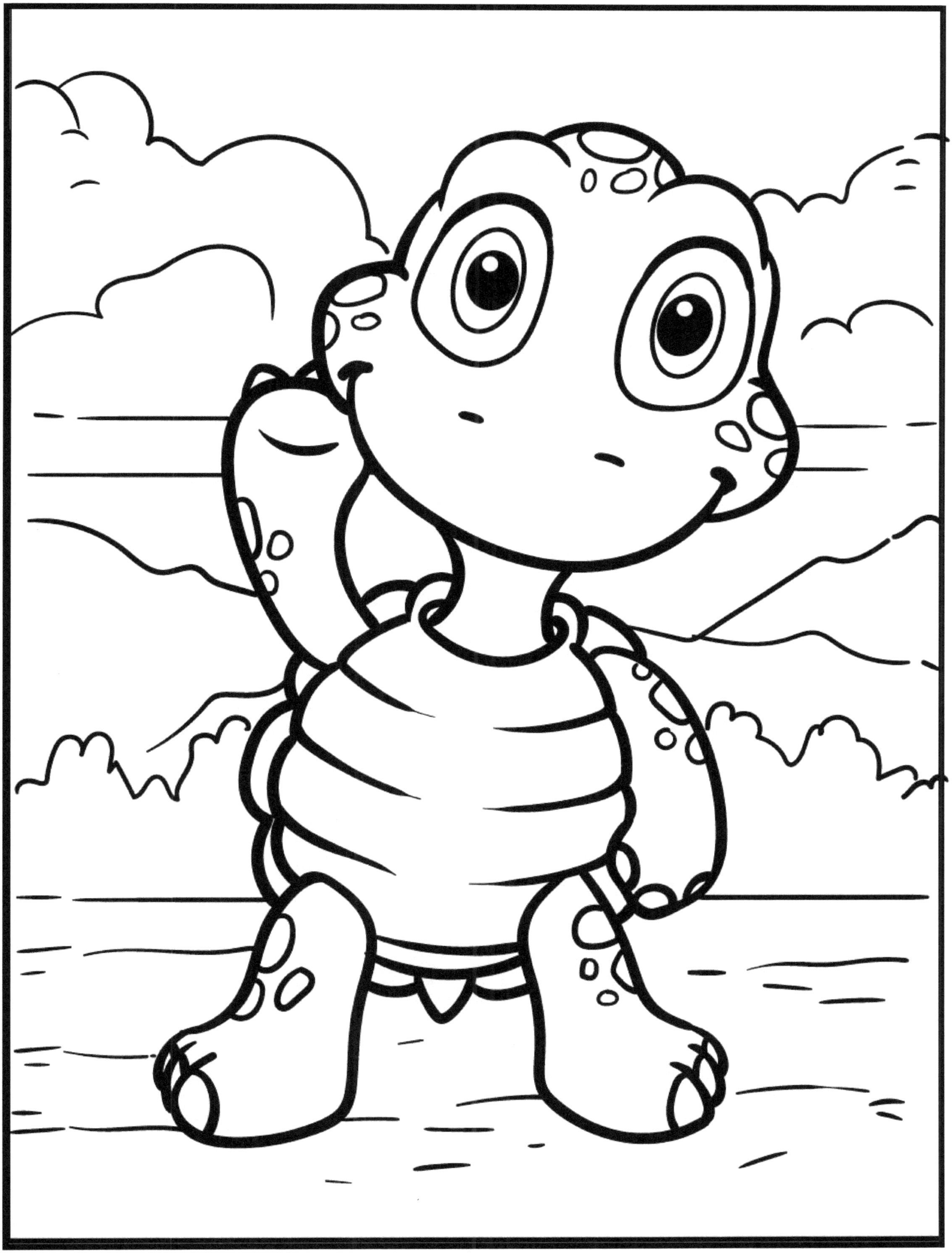

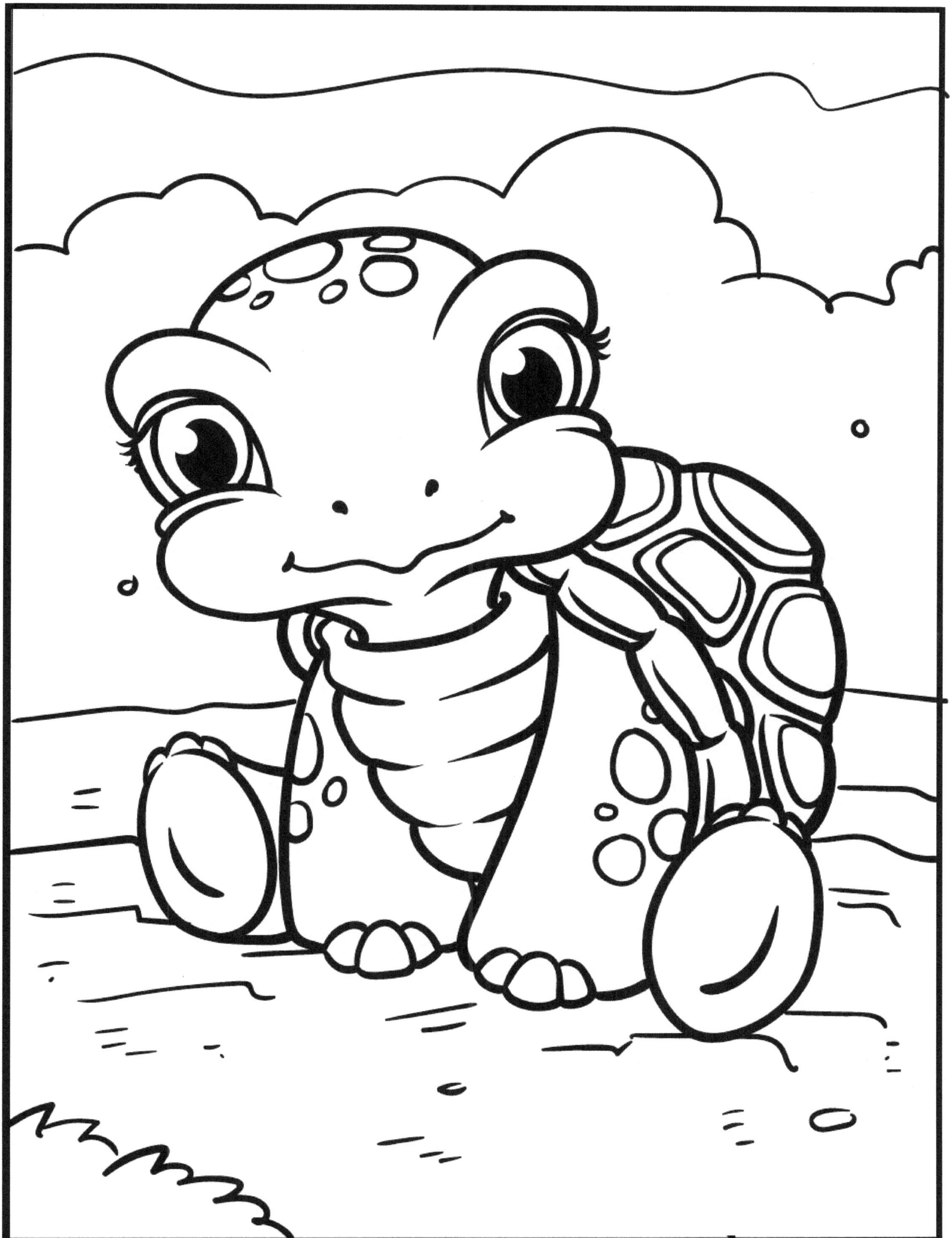

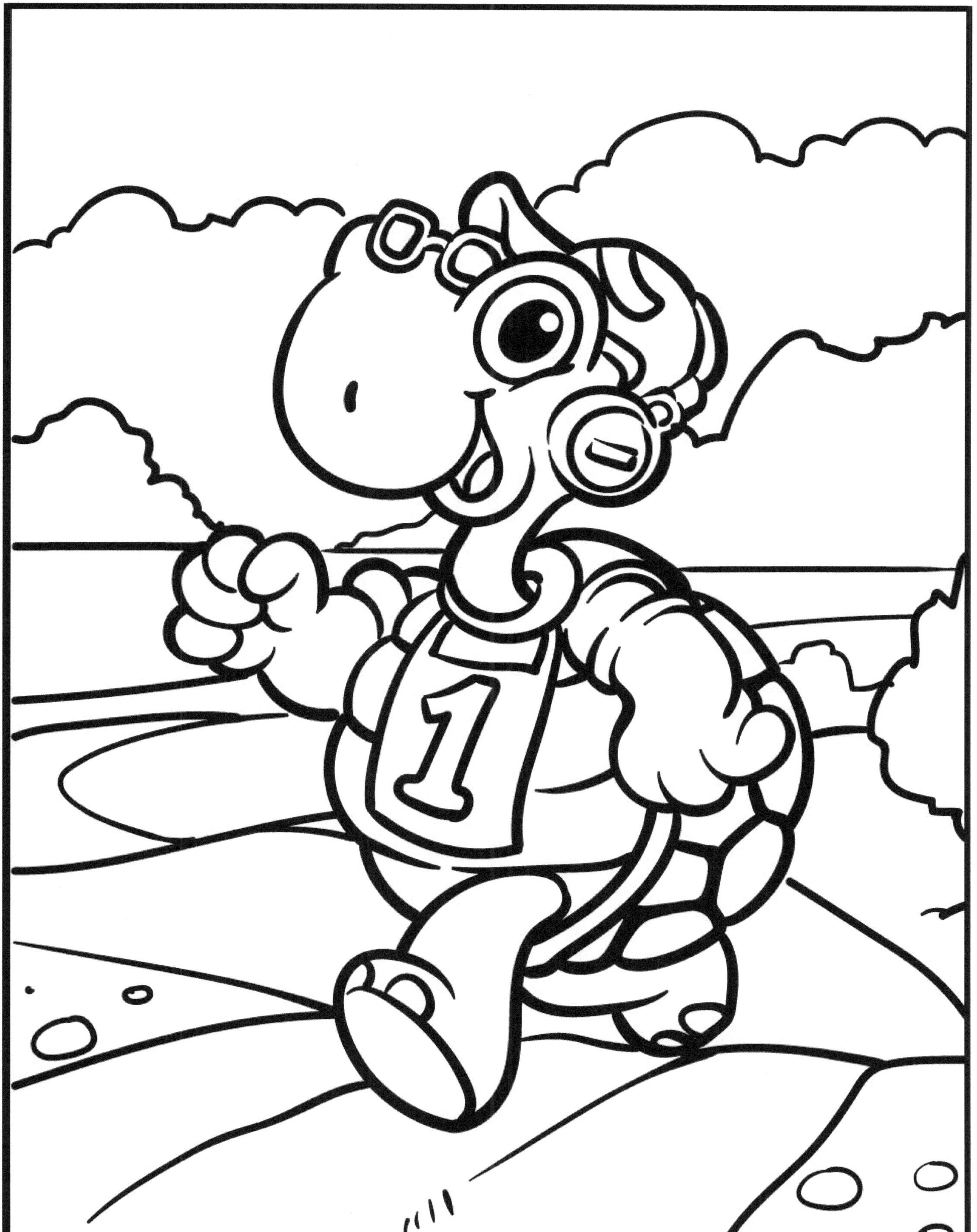
1

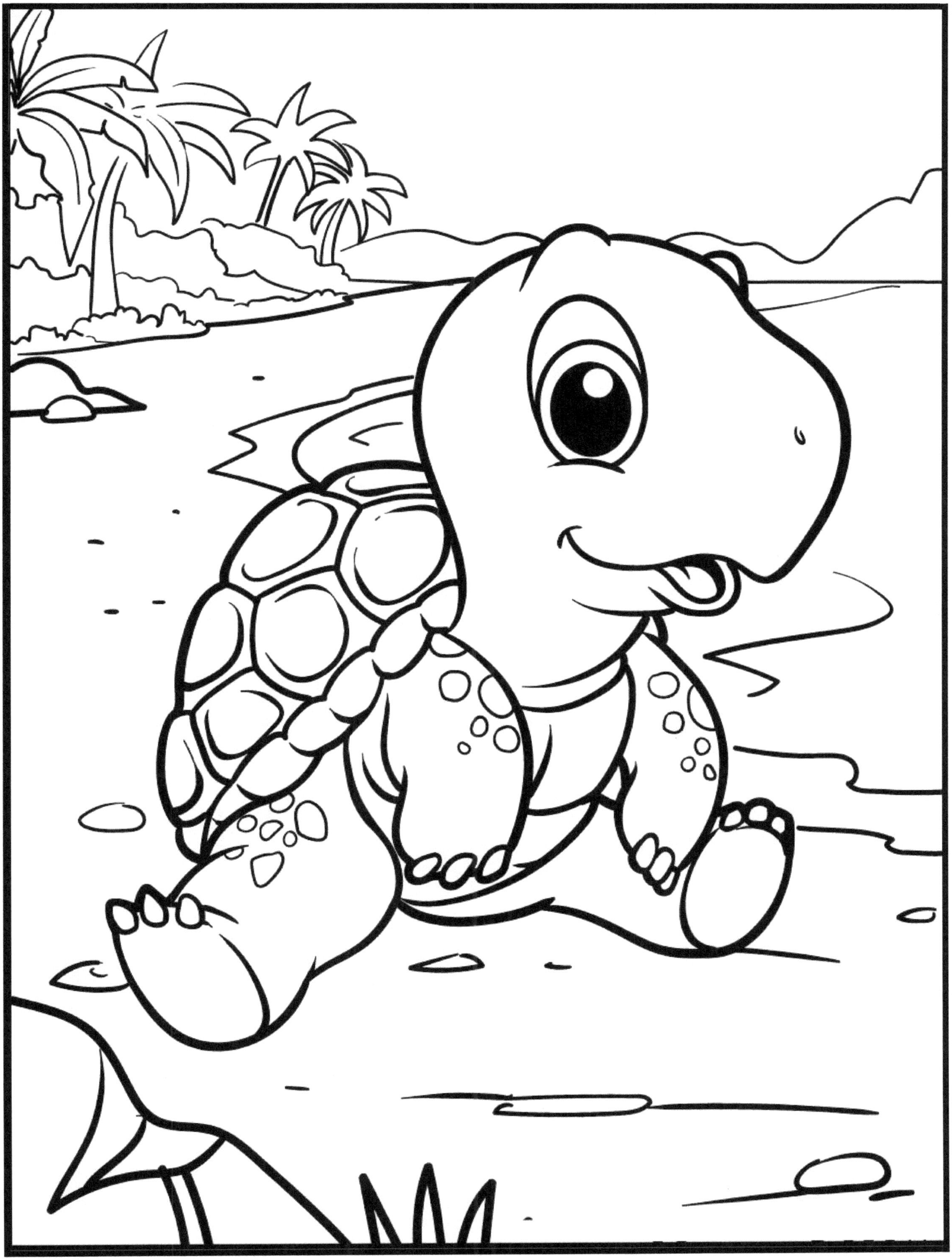

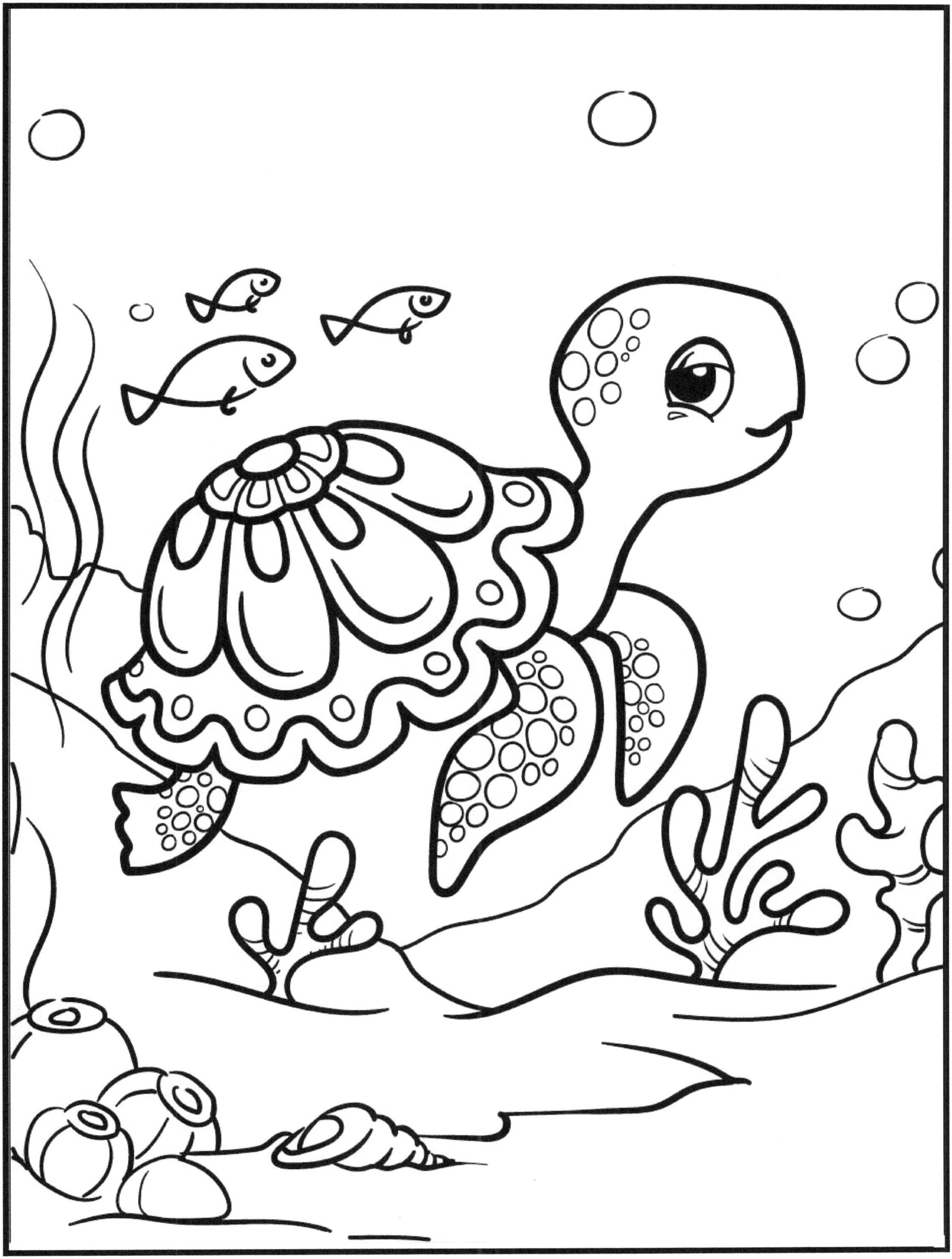

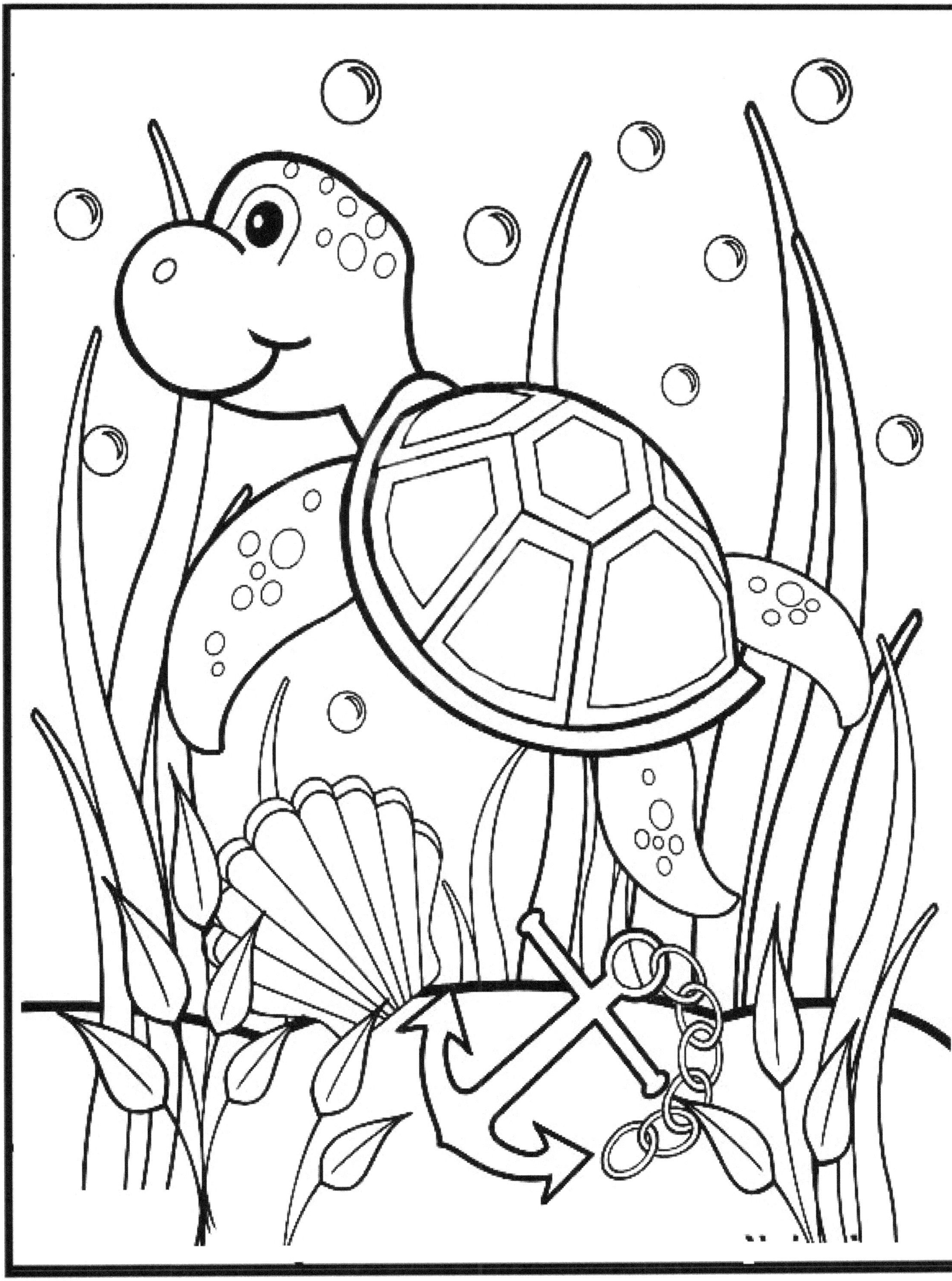

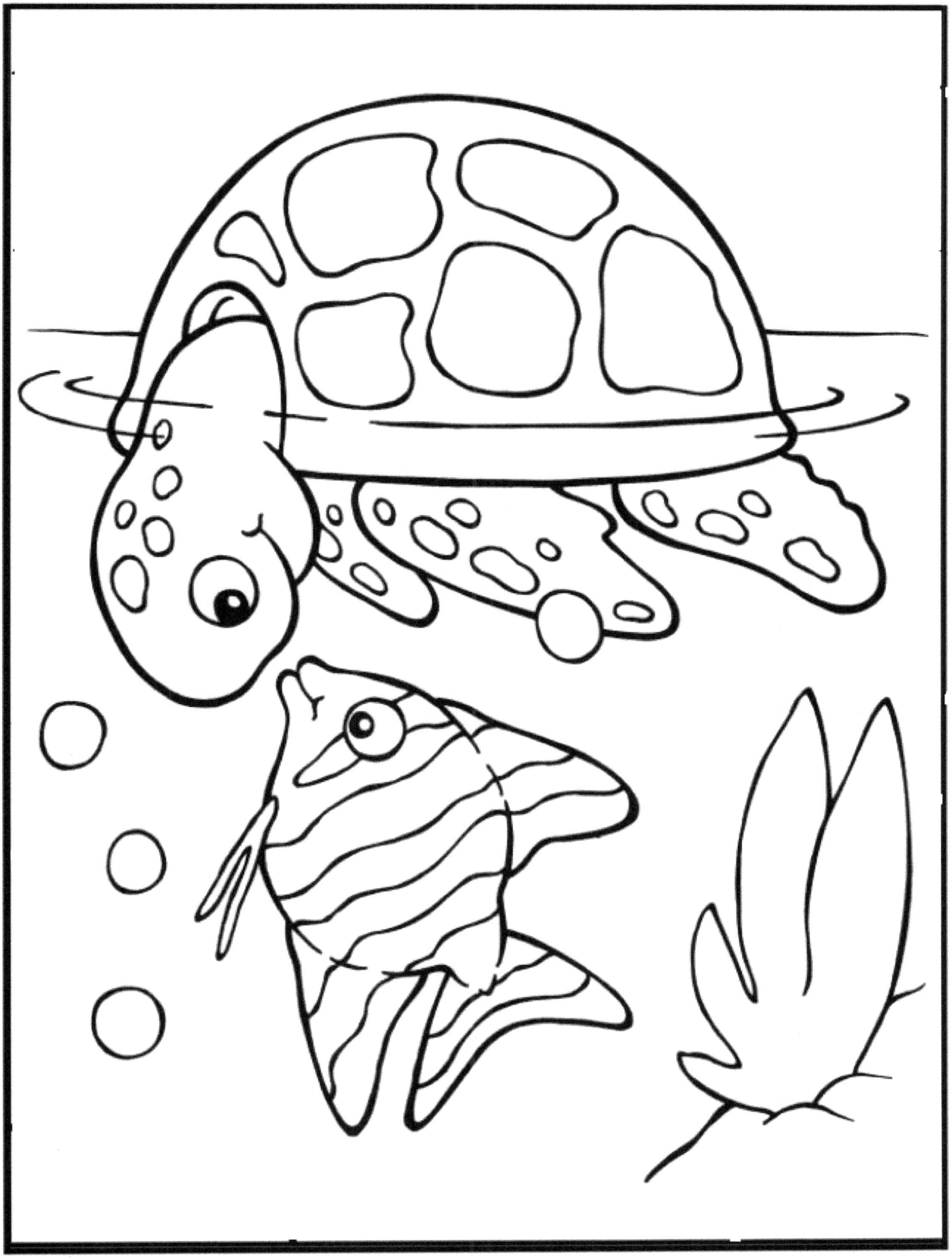

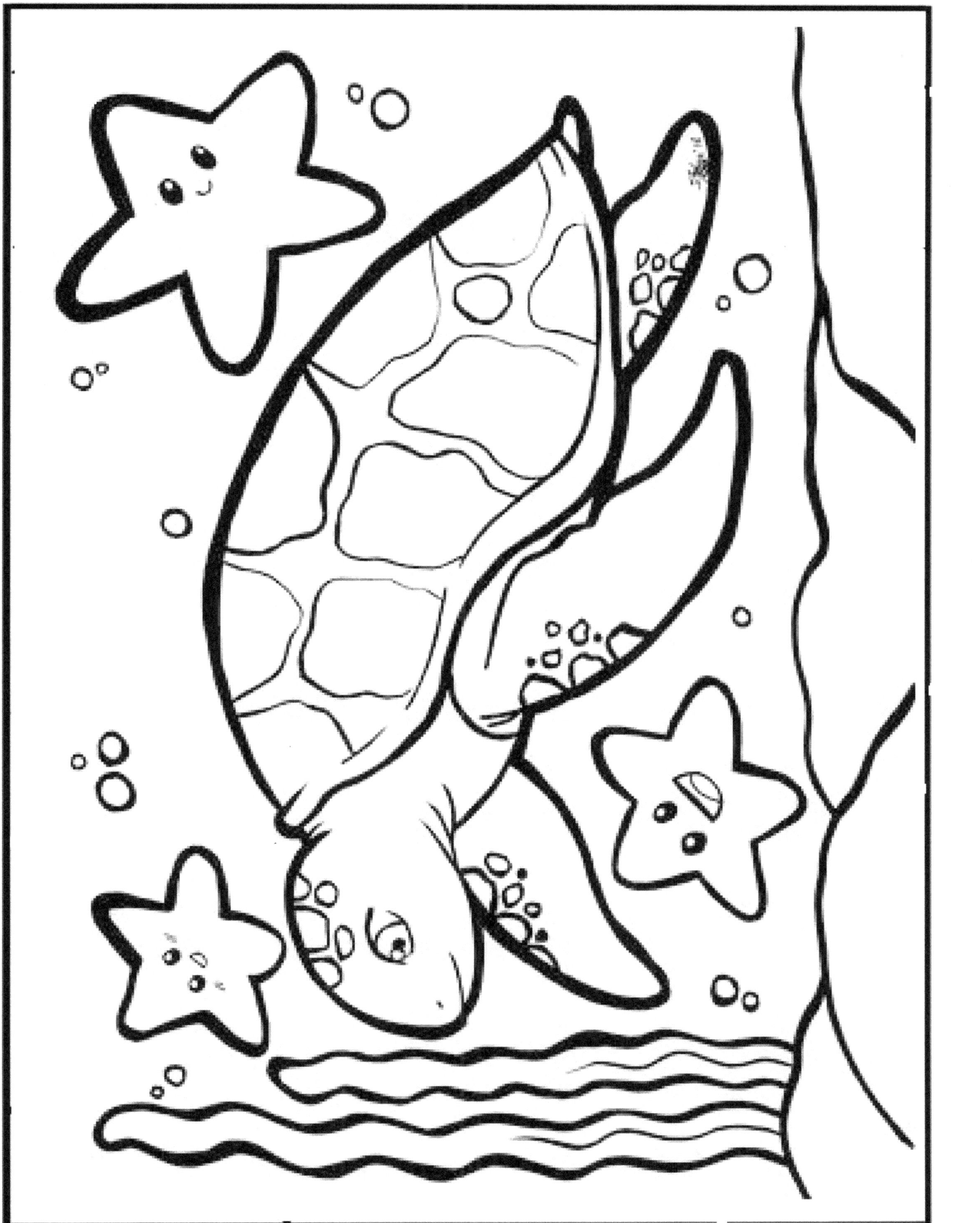

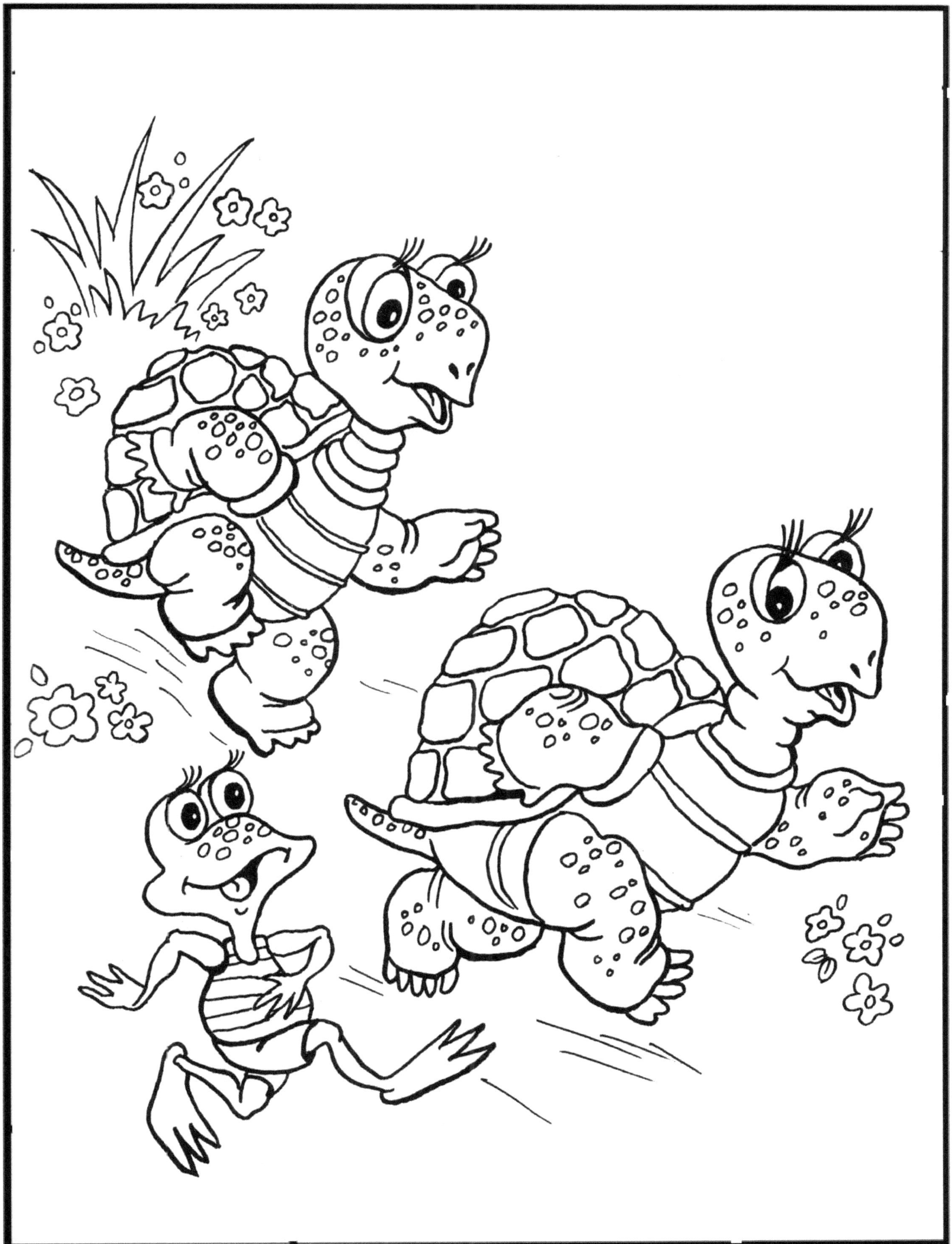

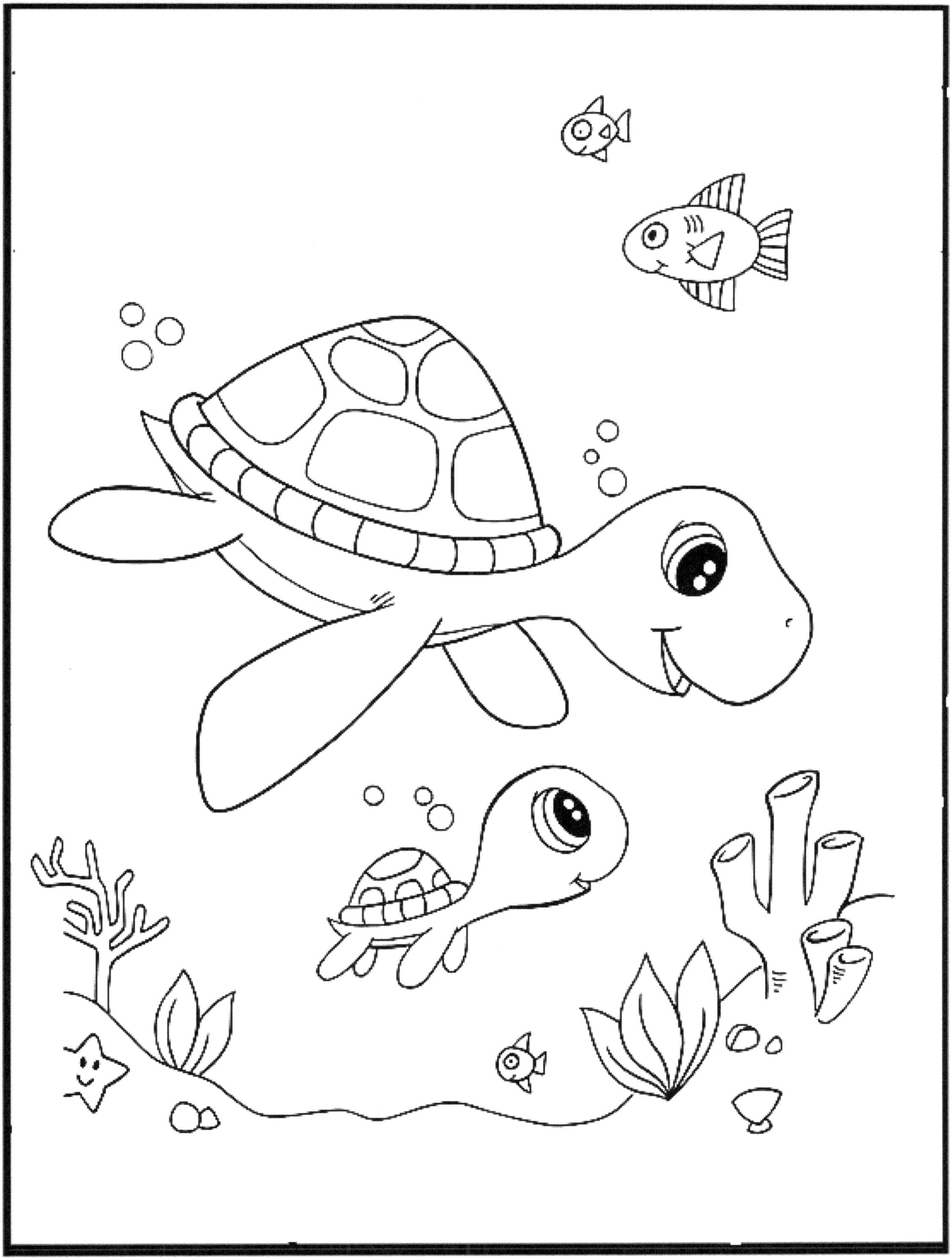

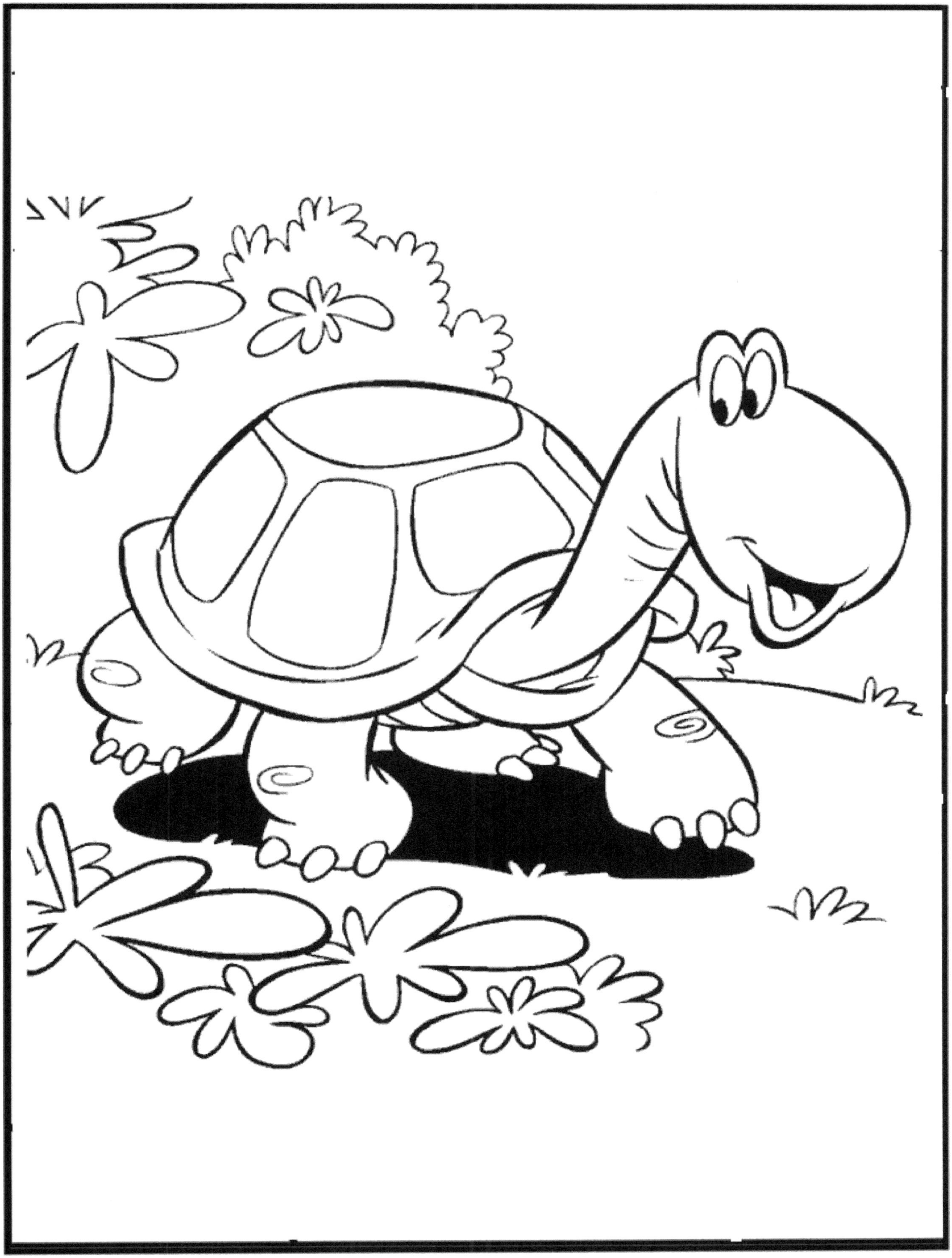

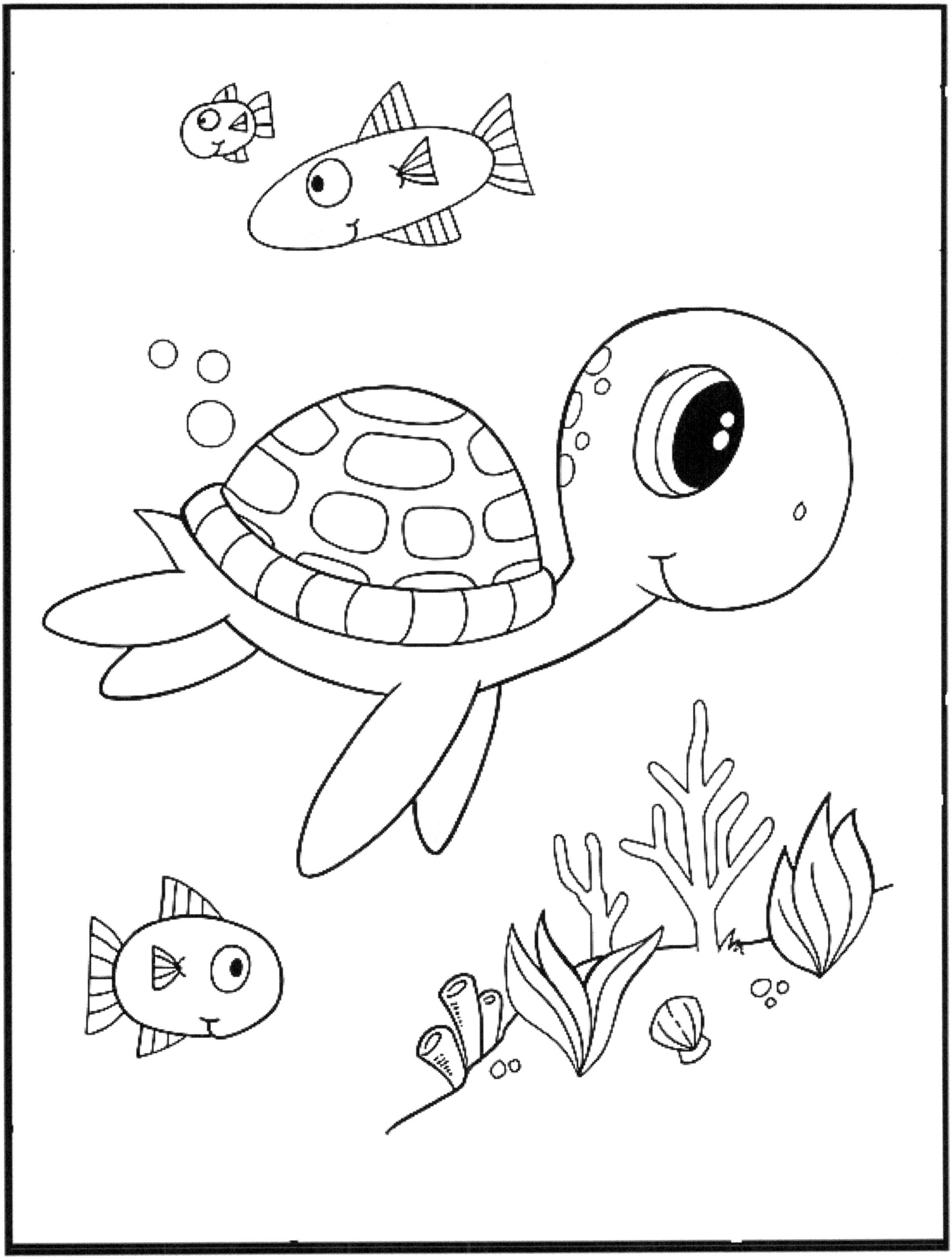

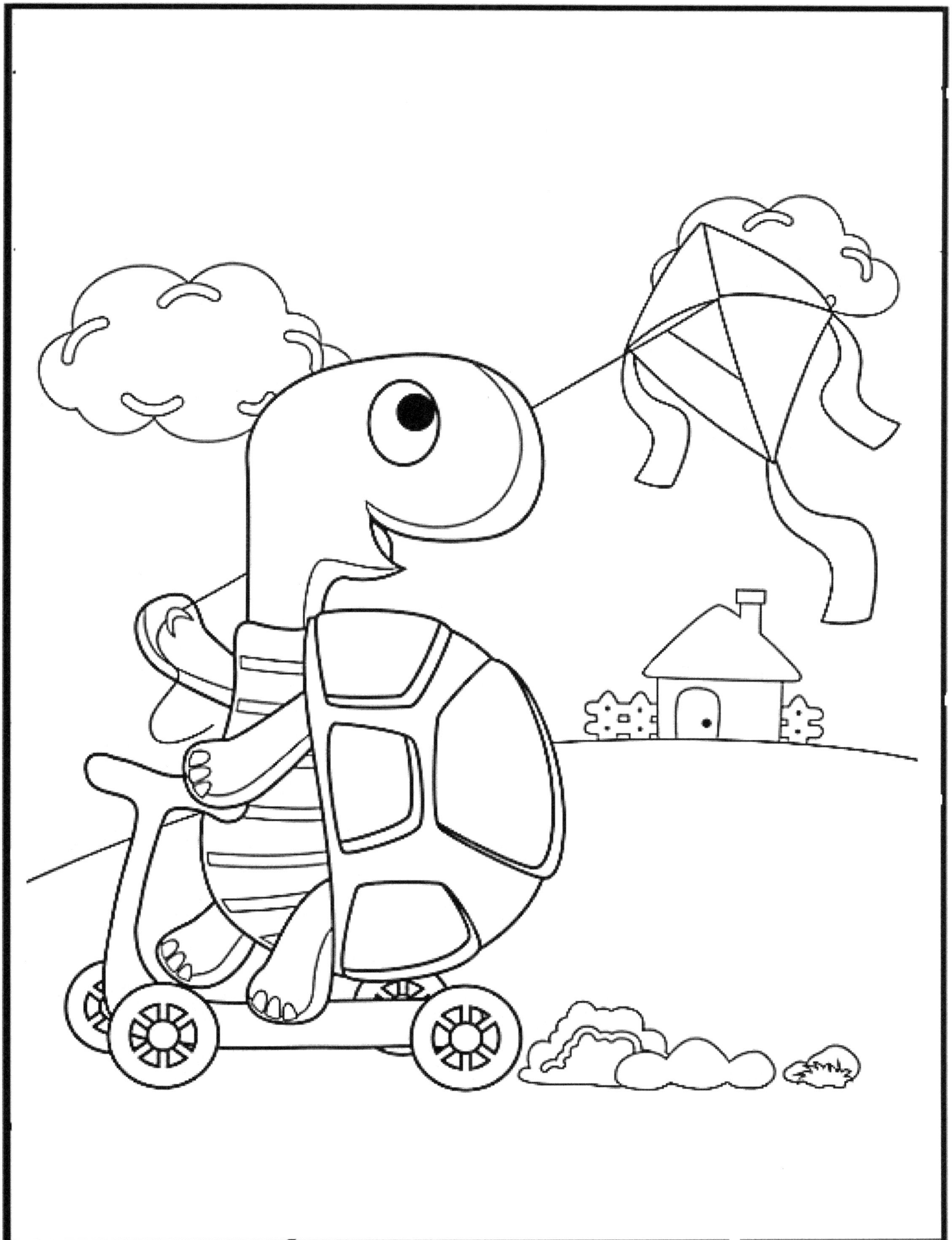

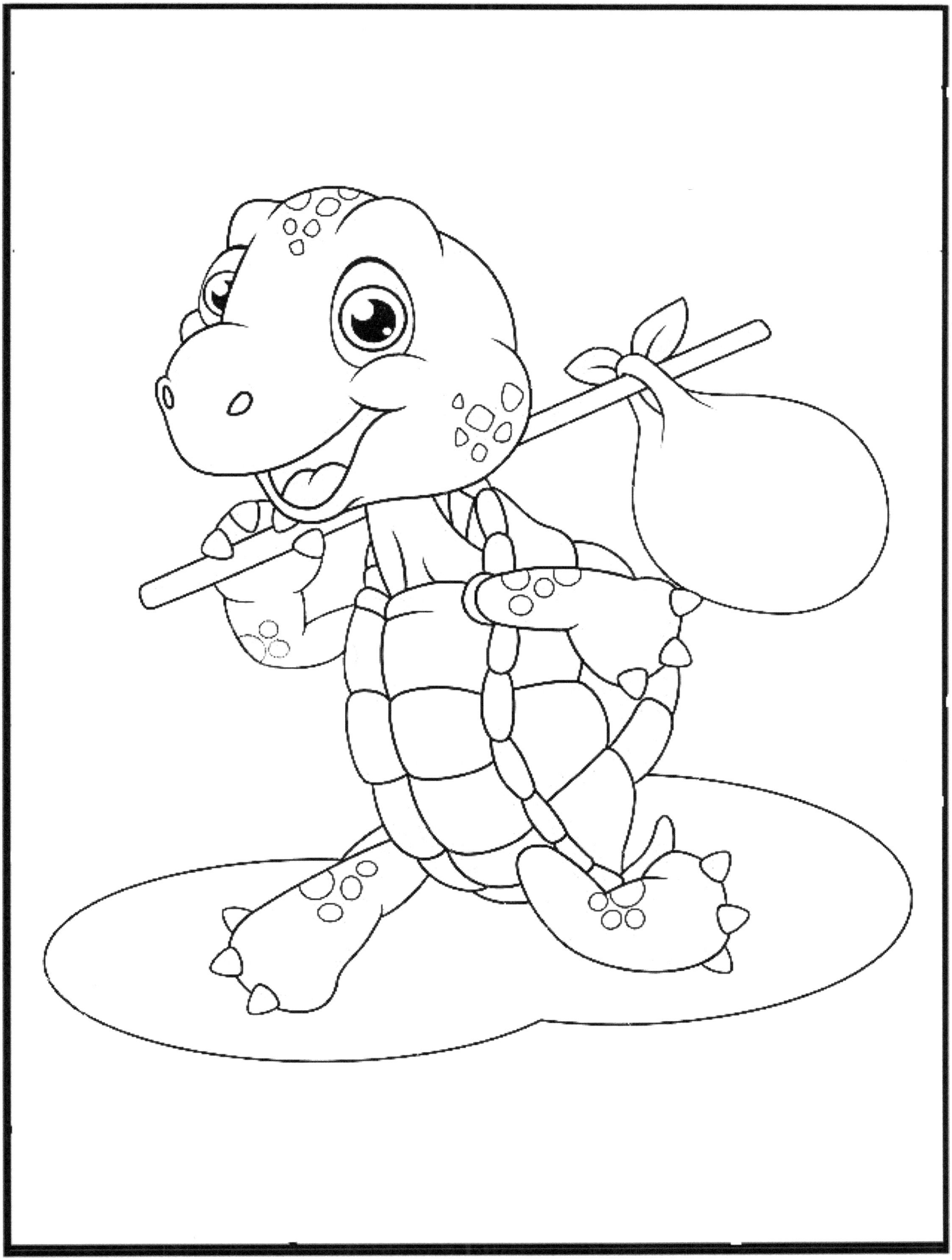

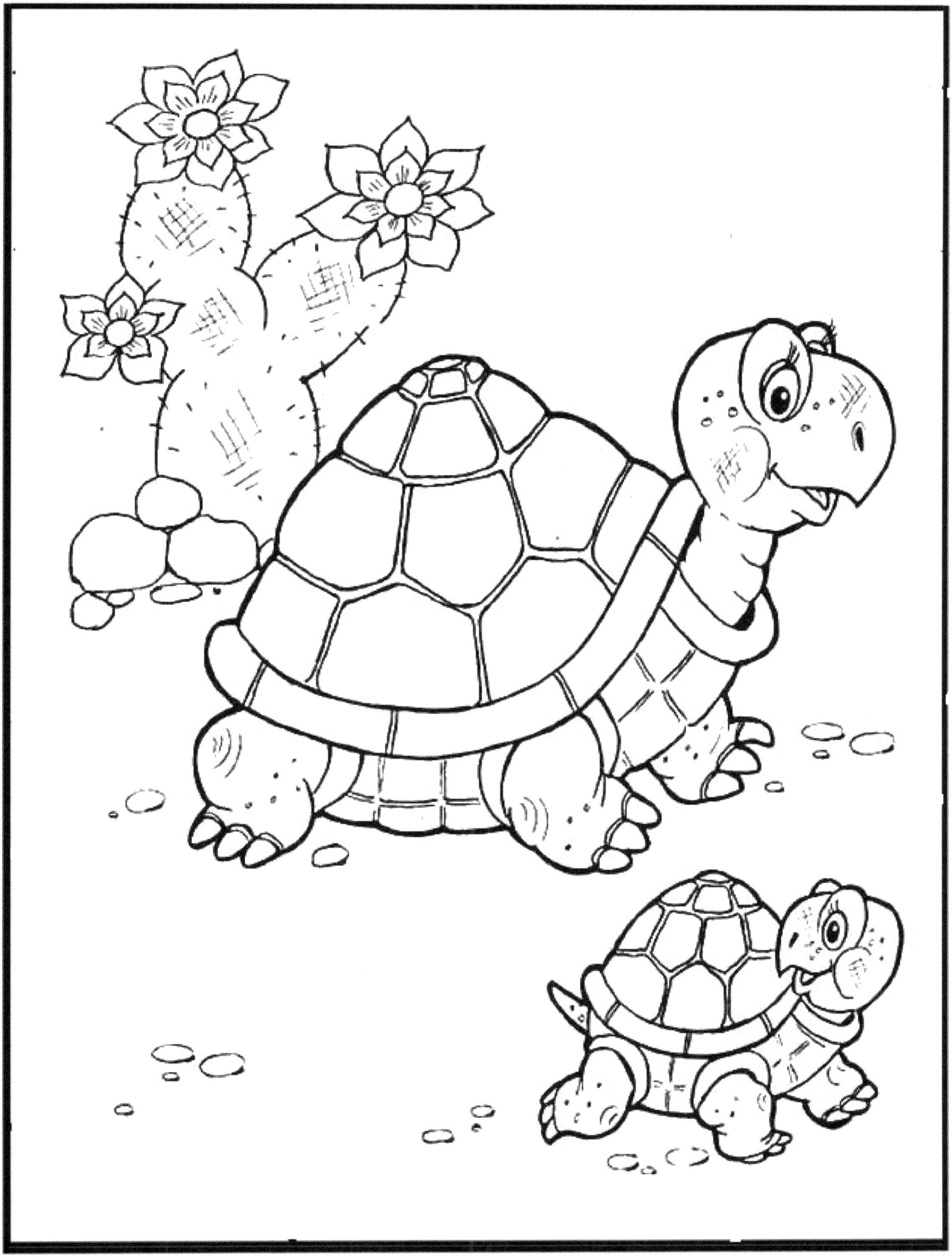

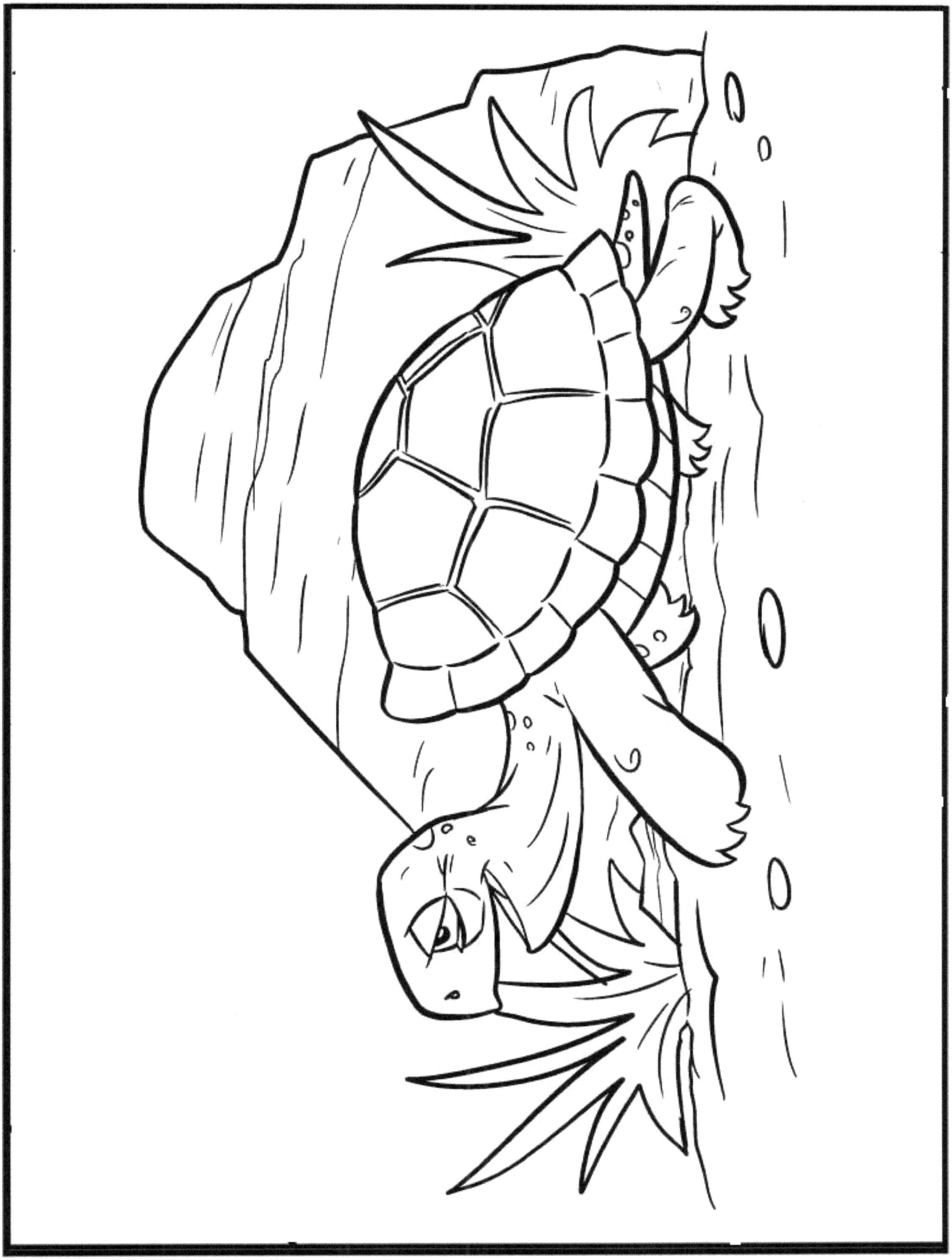

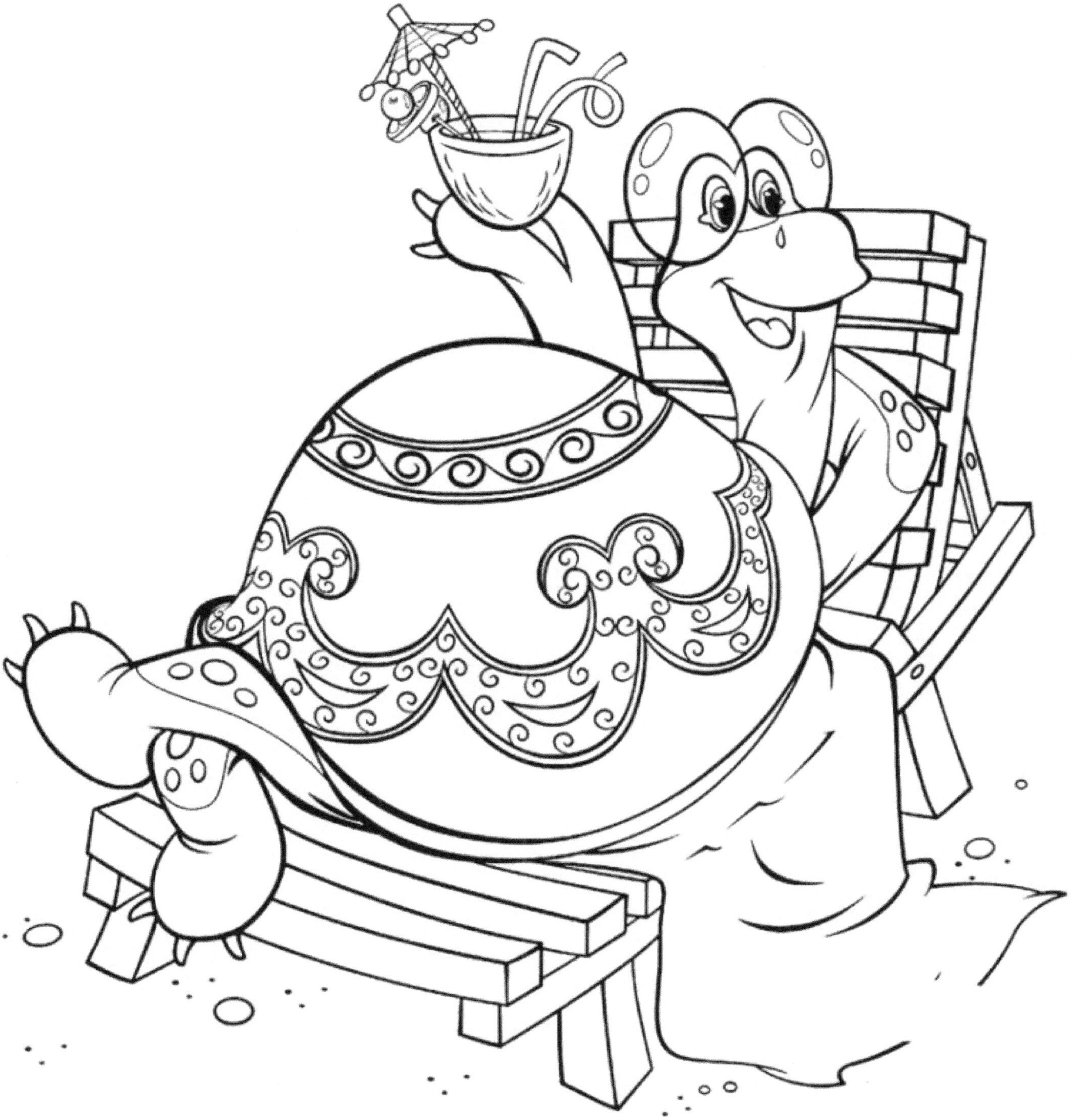

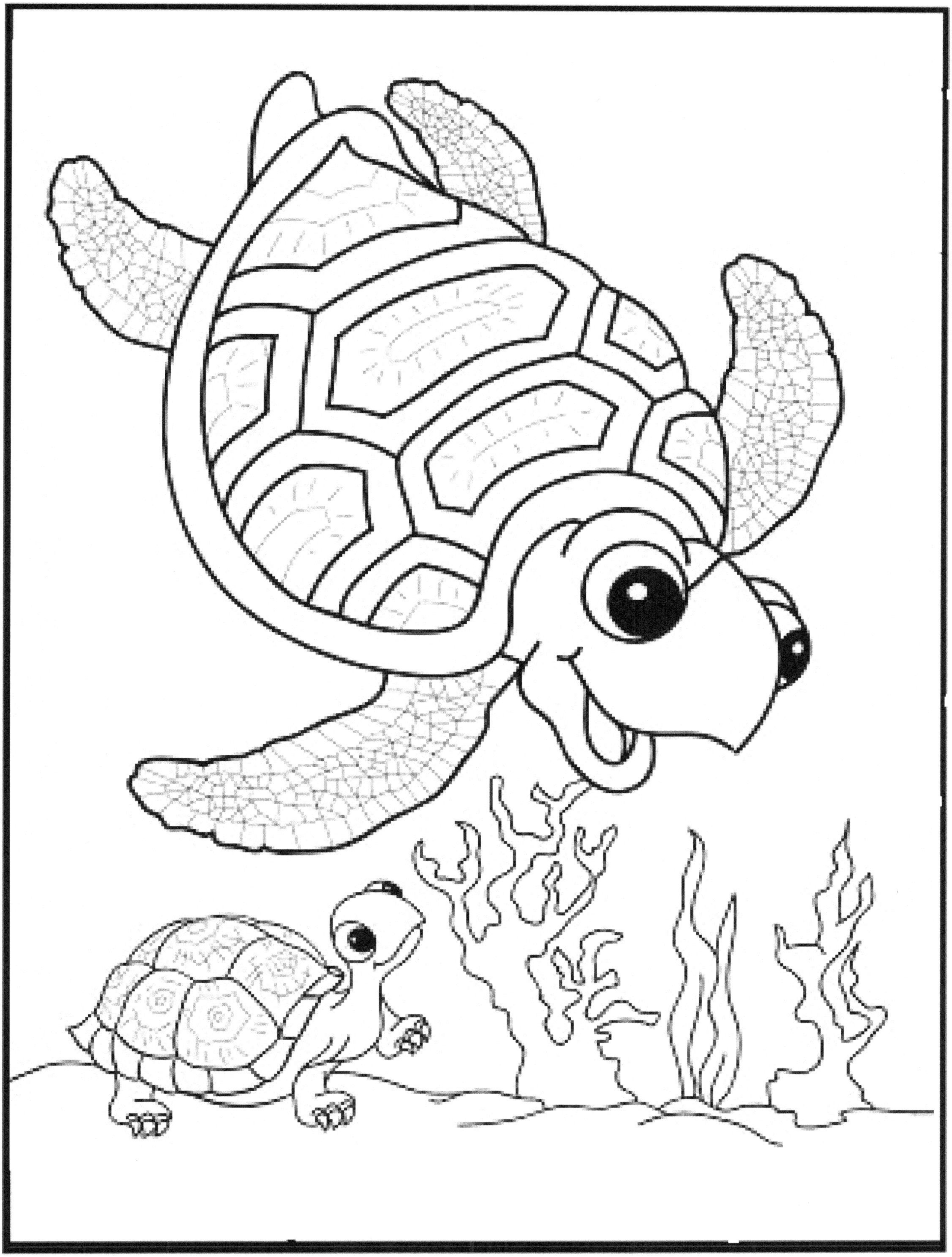

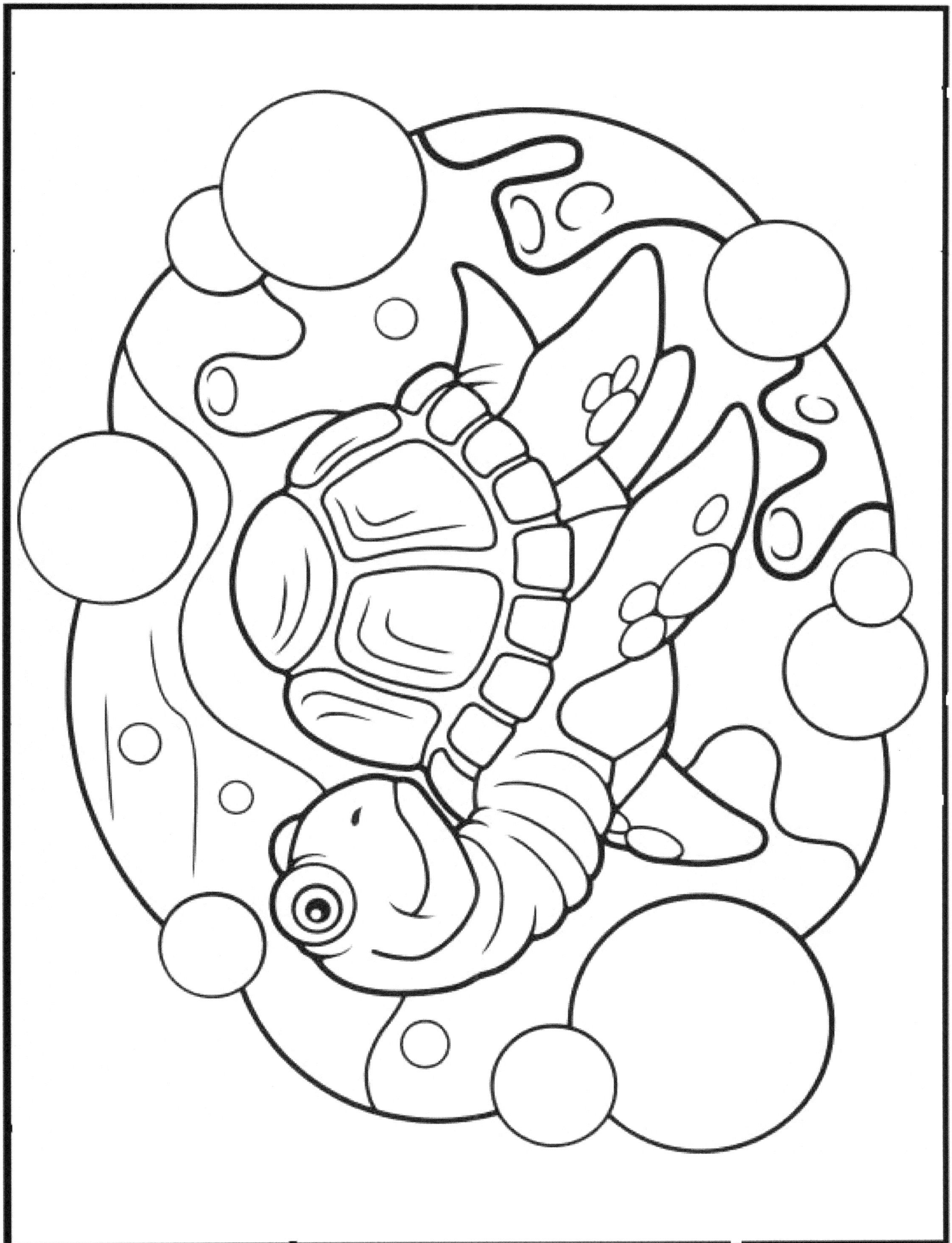

www.ingramcontent.com/pod-product-compliance
Lightning Source LLC
LaVergne TN
LVHW081544060526
838200LV00048B/2202
9781639988013